RICHARD DOYLE'S *JOURNAL*
1840

Richard Doyle's
JOURNAL
1840

Introduction and Notes by
Christopher Wheeler

JOHN BARTHOLOMEW & SON LTD
in association with
BRITISH MUSEUM PUBLICATIONS LTD

First published 1980 by
John Bartholomew & Son Ltd.
12 Duncan Street, Edinburgh EH9 1TA
in association with
British Museum Publications Ltd.
6 Bedford Square, London WC1B 3RA

British Library Cataloguing in Publication Data

Doyle, Richard, *b. 1824*
Richard Doyle's journal.
1. London – Social life and customs
1. Title
942.1'081'0924   DA688

ISBN 0-7028-8280-1

Book and jacket design: Douglas Martin Associates, Leicester
Set in 'Monotype' Baskerville 11/18 by John Swain & Son (Glasgow) Ltd.

Printed in Great Britain by Unwin Brothers Limited,
Old Woking, Surrey

CONTENTS

Introduction

vii

A Note on the *Journal* and this Edition

xvii

The *Journal*

I

Notes

153

INTRODUCTION

This remarkable journal was kept throughout 1840 by a 15-year-old boy, Richard Doyle, largely as a record of his daily life. Within three years he was working for the newly-formed *Punch* and had begun a career that very quickly established him as one of England's leading illustrators, in the same league as 'Phiz' (Hablot K. Browne) and John Leech. As well as his *Punch* work, he undertook commissions to illustrate for some of the principal writers of the day: Dickens, Thackeray, Ruskin, to name just a few; and he also produced books wholly his own: some of his later *Punch* material, modified, appeared with great success in this form. His work and name are no longer as widely known as, say, Phiz's or Tenniel's, or even Leech's, but, for much of his life at any rate, his contemporaries ranked him highly: even in their early, struggling days the Pre-Raphaelite brotherhood carefully set aside money to buy *Punch* for the sake of his work.

The adolescent *Journal* presages the adult fame. It is ably, often amusingly, written, but as might be expected the chief distinction lies in the sketches spread generously through its pages. Their standard is precociously high. Richard was encouraged to continue – and almost certainly to start – the *Journal* by his father, John. He could hardly have had a more suitable mentor. John Doyle, behind the pseudonymous signature 'HB', had begun producing his *Political Sketches* in 1829 for the Haymarket publisher Maclean and, benefiting from growing popular disenchantment with the 'excesses' of Regency caricature, soon established a considerable reputation for his "polite points of wit".[1] All John Doyle's sons inherited this talent

---

1. Thackeray's phrase, used in the *Westminster Review*, June 1840, and quoted in Graham Everitt, *English Caricaturists and Graphic Humourists of the Nineteenth Century* (2nd edn., 1893), p. 240.

for drawing but Richard, the second eldest, was the most accomplished: he had, his father claimed with both pride and justice, "a most ready pencil, a singularly original fancy".[2] Richard, like his father, was never formally taught how to use his skills: he might ultimately have become a better artist if he had been, but he might too have lost the informal, unselfconscious style that makes the *Journal*'s illustrations so delightful.

The Doyles lived in London, at 17 Cambridge Terrace,[3] just off the Edgware Road. Life was well suited to projects such as the *Journal*. None of the children went to school – the most they had to endure was a tutor, Mr Street, calling a few times a week, and occasionally (though not occasionally enough for Richard) dancing lessons from Mr Harbour in the terrace opposite. There was plenty of spare time. Richard used much of his sketching or painting, not without an entrepreneur's eye: borrowing money from his father, he arranged to have his 'Eglinton Tournament' printed.[4] Like many beginners, he was not over-sanguine: "there is something pleasant and important in paying a printer's bill, but nothing in paying a debt to Papa. . . . But supposing I don't get any more sold, then what will I do [?]" His fear was unfounded: he sold the original 50 and had to order more; and even Count D'Orsay, he was enthralled to learn, saw a copy. This success led to another, a commission from Fores's, print-sellers in Piccadilly, to produce a series of designs for illustrated envelopes. The work was not easy – at first Richard did not grasp the technique for drawing on lithographic paper – but when they were ready *The Times* praised them enthusiastically, far above those officially produced for the Post Office by William Mulready.

The Doyles were a close-knit, slightly inward-looking family. John Doyle and his wife, Marianna, had come to London from Dublin in the 1820s, bringing with them a

2. In a letter to Sir Robert Peel (22 January 1842), Add MSS BM 40500, Peel Papers, f. 318.
3. The terrace still stands as the east end of Sussex Gardens; the original numbering has not survived.
4. This 'tournament', a romantic recreation of the medieval event, was held at Eglinton Castle on the Ayrshire coast in August 1839, at immense expense to its sponsor, the Earl of Eglinton. Disraeli describes it in *Endymion*.

staunch Irish Catholicism that must sometimes have made it difficult for them to mix easily with those of a different – or weaker – persuasion. The Cambridge Terrace address was shared with Marianna's brother Michael Conan and his wife, though possibly not till after the premature death, a few years before the *Journal*, of Marianna. It is difficult to gauge precisely how 'well off' the family was: John Doyle faintly complained that his publisher was "much the larger gainer" from the success of his *Political Sketches*,[5] but this is a conventional grumble and probably need not be taken too seriously; certainly the *Journal* suggests a life lived in reasonable comfort, in a terrace of good quality, if not high fashion, close to the pleasures of Hyde Park and, not far beyond, open country. Entertaining was by and large restricted to a small circle of friends, but the occasions do not seem to have been dull: some 50 years later Charles Doyle – the youngest child – was still able to recall animated drawing-room discussions on religion and politics, listened to, often till one or two in the morning, from his bedroom above.[6] Outings were frequent: to the opera, concerts, Regent's Park Zoo, the Tower of London. Visits to exhibitions and galleries, to painters and sculptors themselves if arrangements could be made, were common: the Royal Academy and National Gallery feature prominently in the pages of this journal.

Richard sketched his impressions of these events. Also, of course, of household life. Military parades and drills, too, are well recorded: Richard was an avid spectator. Occasionally his sketches unwittingly provide less obvious glimpses of early-Victorian London: usually no more than small details, but *in*formal views are rare in this still pre-photographic age.[7] Even the humblest artist was not often required to treat the commonplaces of life. What artist, had he seen it, would have troubled to record the trickery of an Oxford Street trader (p. 121), no doubt only too familiar a sight? Yet it is a marvellous scene: a gullible crowd gathering as this man offers

5. Add MSS BM 40500, Peel Papers, f. 318.
6. Charles Altamont Doyle, *The Doyle Diary*, ed. Michael Baker (1978), p. 15.
7. The Daguerrotype was already invented (1839) and indeed was exhibited at the Polytechnic Institution visited by Richard (pp. 48–9), though he seems not to have seen it; but for all practical purposes 1840 was still 'pre-photographic'.

'silver' rings for sale at 1d. each; an old woman, quite oblivious to it all, crouching down smoking a pipe and skinning fish; a waiter from one of the Oxford Street inns carrying a large joint of meat, possibly ordered for a club near by, certainly growing cold as he dallies to see what is happening; behind him a figure with what might be a grinding wheel for sharpening knives; and at the extreme right of the illustration a figure in crumpled hat and dishevelled dress leaning, perhaps drunkenly, on a post. Similarly, the interior of Ackermann's print-shop in the Strand (p. 113) or, say, the booking-hall of Paddington Station (p. 45) are perfectly 'ordinary', casual scenes – and interesting now for precisely that reason. Ackermann's shows an almost domestic cosiness, with a minimum of shop-fittings and many of the wares laid out on tables covered with tablecloths. Lamps, perhaps colza rather than gas, hang from the ceiling, framed prints hang on the wall – a few, loose, lie scattered on the floor – the décor itself is simple and restrained: the whole scene is a reminder that though strictly Victorian London appears in this journal its features are often still Georgian or Regency. An obvious exception is the emergent railway system, glimpsed in several of Richard's sketches. One of these, accompanying Richard's description of his train ride to Ealing, is the buying of tickets at Paddington: it shows not the expected ticket booth, a feature generally thought to be as old as the stations themselves, but an open table.[8] Was this a usual practice on the early railways or simply a reflection of the slightly makeshift nature of the Great Western Railway's first London terminus?

Not quite all the *Journal*'s illustrations are in this key. Some are much grander. Victoria was married in 1840 and Richard, in common with others this time, sketched his impressions of the royal drive to and from Westminster Abbey; considering the size of the crowd, his height (5 ft), and the difficulty of getting past "old women with coal scuttle bonnets and green umbrellas", he did well to manage. A sketch of the royal coach and its occupants is naturally prominent in his entry (p. 20), but he is also interested in the crowd, in incidental detail such as the

8. I am grateful to Professor Jack Simmons for this point.

Life-Guard's rearing horse (p. 18); woodcuts of the drive in the next day's news-papers, detailed and conventional, convey little of the excitement evidently felt by Richard.

The family group seen in these pages did not survive intact for very much longer: Adelaide, the youngest daughter, died of consumption in 1844; Francis, too, the third son, died within a few years, possibly of the same disease. Among the children, this left James, Richard, Henry, Charles, and Annette. All the sons had a talent for drawing and more or less used it in their subsequent careers,[9] but Richard outshone the rest and only he lived by illustration alone. Success was quick to come his way: a couple of years after the Fores commission Bentley asked him to provide a few sketches for Maxwell's *Hector O'Halloran*, to accompany others drawn by John Leech; but most decisively of all, he was introduced to *Punch*'s editor Mark Lemon and, at 18, taken on to the paper's staff. He did not start auspiciously. *Punch*'s engraver, Swain, was asked to instruct Richard in the technique of drawing on wood, but "so nervous was the youth, who was small and thin in person, and greatly agitated in mind and manner, that he persisted in keeping his distance out of simple shyness, and literally dodged around the dining-room table, altogether too excited to lend the slightest attention to the words of his mentor".[10] This difficulty was evidently overcome for by the following year he was proficient enough to design *Punch* a new cover. It is a measure of his ability that this, the *sixth* design since the paper's first appearance in 1841, lasted, with some modification in 1849, until well

9. James (1822–92) began as a painter, but soon turned to history instead. He wrote *A Chronicle of England* (1864), containing 81 coloured illustrations, and *The Official Baronage of England* (1886, 3 vols.), with some 1,000 illustrations. Henry (1827–92) started his career as a draughtsman and wood-engraver; in 1844 he made a number of small cuts for *Punch* and from 1867 to 1869 did the cartoons for *Fun*. He painted a few portraits but his preference was for religious art. In 1869 he became Director of the National Gallery of Ireland. Charles (1832–93), father of Sir Arthur Conan Doyle, worked for most of his life in the Edinburgh Office of Works; he contributed a few illustrations to *London Society* and a few of his paintings were exhibited at the Royal Scottish Academy.

10. M. H. Spielmann, *The History of 'Punch'* (1895), p. 454.

into our own century. Much of his work was decorative – initial letters, vignettes, head and tail pieces – but he also contributed a considerable number of full-scale cartoons. He was never *Punch*'s principal artist – John Leech held that position – but his work was popular, particularly the humorous series 'Manners and Customs of Ye Englyshe', which viewed contemporary society as through a medieval tapestry, and 'Brown, Jones, and Robinson', tales of three hapless young bachelors. A slightly expanded form of 'Manners and Customs' was later published as a book and 'Brown, Jones, and Robinson' formed the kernel of *The Foreign Tour of Brown, Jones, and Robinson* (1854).

Richard also worked in these years as a book illustrator. Dickens employed him for some of the illustrations in the *Christmas Books*, though characteristically Dickens was difficult to please: he first saw the designs for *The Chimes* at a Covent Garden coffee house and thought two – one Doyle's, the other by Leech – quite unsuitable. "I had them both to breakfast with me this morning", he wrote to his wife, Kate, "and with that winning manner which you know of, got them with the highest good humour to do both afresh".[11] A few commissions in this period, Grimm's *The Fairy Ring*, for example, suggest Richard's delight in drawing fanciful figures from the elf world, a pleasure freely indulged in the pages of this journal, and also the path of much of his later work, from *The King of the Golden River*, a fairy-tale written by Ruskin for his wife Effie, to *In Fairyland* and beyond.

On the whole the 1840s seem to have been years of reasonable contentment for Richard: after 1842 he had a secure job, probably not badly paid, his cloistered adolescent years gave way to a great deal of social activity, in company with some of the foremost writers and artists of the time – drinking burnt sherry and eating anchovy toast with Dickens in Fleet Street's Rainbow Tavern[12] would have been

11. Walter Dexter, ed., Nonesuch Edition of *The Letters of Charles Dickens* (3 vols., 1938), I, p. 647, quoted in Robert L. Patten, *Charles Dickens and his Publishers* (1978), p. 160.

12. Described in a letter from Richard to Charles beginning "I have been nearly worked to death" (n.d., from a collection of typed copies of Richard's letters held by the Département des Manuscrits, Bibliothèque Cantonale et Universitaire, Lausanne. Another collection exists, in England, but at time of writing is the subject of a lawsuit and not available for inspection).

beyond the wildest dreams of the *Journal*'s Richard. But he never lost his shyness and reserve – at the *Punch* dinners, lively and sometimes boisterous affairs, he was a 'listener' rather than one of the main protagonists; and several contemporaries refer to his silence in company, even if individually he could be charming and entertaining. Holman Hunt meeting Richard at the end of the decade later wrote a brief description of the occasion: "I also met the unique and delightful Richard Doyle, a man overflowing with witty stories but with never a word of uncharitableness, who from this time became my prized friend until his life's end. He was standing leaning against the wall, crush hat in hand, one leg crossing the other. He was still quite young, and his face spoke a happy mixture of interest and humour."[13] Even though this is the recollection of an old friend, there is no reason to doubt the essential impression of easy-going geniality. But it is not a complete view. Like his father, he took his adherence to Catholicism very seriously. Many of his letters reveal this. In 1850 this strength of belief led to his resignation from *Punch*.

The break came not because *Punch* joined in the attack on 'Papal Aggression' – a decision by Rome to re-establish in England an ecclesiastical hierarchy, for the first time since Henry VIII's Act of Supremacy – but because in doing so it personally insulted the Pope; this was more than Richard was prepared to tolerate, as Mark Lemon might have appreciated in advance had he seen the entry on pp. 136 –7 of this journal: "as I was crossing Berkley square on my way to the British Gallery lo an imposing sight presents itself, a Guy placed gracefully upon the back of a donkey back to back with a novel creature who might have passed for some distant relation of Punch, or even Judy, but was I believe intended to represent the Pope. The sarcasm here conveyed was so biting that I quitted the ground instantly". One contemporary rumour, originating it seems with the publisher Murray, had it that Richard was forced to resign under the threat of excommunication;[14] this passage suggests that such pressure, most unlikely anyway, would have been entirely superfluous.

13. Holman Hunt, *Pre-Raphaelitism and the Pre-Raphaelite Brotherhood* (2 vols., 1905), I, pp. 273–4.
14. Marion Lockhead, *John Gibson Lockhart* (1954), pp. 283–4.

The break with *Punch* drew a distinct line across Richard Doyle's career. He was still young – only 26 – and his illustrations were well liked, his name well known, but he lost a regular source of income and, worst of all, his audience. He was offered various commissions, but not all went well: asked to illustrate Swift's humorous works, he gave a principled refusal, not caring greatly for the author's notions of morality; he *did* accept a commission from the Dalziel brothers to produce a *Panorama of an Overland Journey to the Great Exhibition of 1851*, intended to be published before the opening day, but the drawings were not done on time, in fact the last of them was not finished until the close of the exhibition: not surprisingly the publication was a flop. Even by 1853 things do not seem to have improved. Mrs Procter wrote to Thackeray, then in America: "Your friends are well – Richard Doyle cheers up when your name is mentioned – I say 'cheers up' because he looks sad and is doing nothing – and this is a great pity".[15] More than the aftermath of the *Punch* split played on his mind during this period. He was strongly attracted to Blanche Stanley (of the Stanleys of Alderley), a beautiful girl with an extrovert, perhaps slightly mischievous, temperament.[16] He wrote to his brother Charles: "When I tell you . . . that Lady Stanley told me that her daughter . . . would be 'so sorry that she had not been there [at a house party] when she heard I was there' . . . I thought I should have bust . . . . little did that imperious woman and mother know the workings of my innermost soul". Even had Blanche felt similarly – there is no evidence either way – the match would have been 'impossible', as Richard must have realized: not only was he merely an illustrator and cartoonist, however celebrated, he was a Roman Catholic. Still, he would have shown remarkable stoicism not to feel some anguish over her marriage to the Earl of Airlie in 1851, only months after his painful parting from *Punch*.

15. Letter of 8 March 1853 in Gordon N. Ray (ed.), *The Letters and Private Papers of W. M. Thackeray* (4 vols., 1945–6), III, p. 231.

16. In the summer of 1852, following an afternoon spent with Blanche, Mrs Carlyle wrote of her: "I can give . . . no idea of her indiscretion, nor of the charm of beauty and childlikeness that makes one always pardon her". Leonard Huxley (ed.), *Jane Welsh Carlyle: Letters to her Family, 1839–63* (1924), letter 162, quoted in Nancy Mitford (ed.), *The Stanleys of Alderley* (1939), p. 52.

The most substantial commission to come Richard's way in these difficult years
was from Thackeray to illustrate *The Newcomes*. No doubt Thackeray's motives were
mixed: he certainly wanted to help his friend but he also realized – despite occasional
irritated outbursts to suggest the contrary – that Doyle was likely to do the novel
more justice than he ever could: "I have seen for the first time the engravings of
Newcomes some of wh I like very much indeed. Why, Doyle ought to bless the day
that put the etching needle into his hand. I'm sure he'll be able to do great things
with it. He does beautifully and easily what I wanted to do and can't".[17] The ease at
any rate seems to have been deceptive: Richard complained of guess-work involved
in depicting the book's characters: "Thackeray scarcely ever describes a character as
Dickens does, all at once – he leaves them to work themselves out by degrees, so that
after reading the MS [manuscript] of a couple of Numbers one really knows scarcely
anything about the story".[18] One of the characters, though, may have seemed
familiar from the start if we can believe that J. J. Ridley – "the fellow what can draw"
– is in part a pen-portrait of Doyle himself.[19]

Richard continued to illustrate for almost another 30 years after completion of *The
Newcomes*, but the popularity of his work was past its peak; his talents were not
ignored – in 1870 indeed text was commissioned to accompany his illustrations for *In
Fairyland*, not vice versa – but he was no longer the artist of the minute, and the
limitations of his style, unimportant in the pages of *Punch*, became more rather than
less apparent. He never gave up painting and exhibited at both the Royal Academy
and the Grosvenor Galleries; but again his lack of formal training is often painfully
evident, and must have seemed even more so in comparison with the works of many
of the other exhibitors.

It is hard to avoid the feeling that Richard Doyle's later life was tinged with a
slight sadness, a sense of unfulfilment. But the impression should not be pushed to an

17. In a letter to Percival Leigh (12 April 1854). Ray, *op. cit.*, III, p. 362.
18. In a letter from Richard to Charles beginning 'Being Sunday I sit down to very hastily jot you a line'
(n.d., from the Lausanne collection, *op. cit.*).
19. Suggested in Lewis Lusk (pseudonym for W. D. Scull), 'The Art of Richard Doyle' (*c.* 1903), f. 36.
Unpublished MS in the Lausanne collection, *op. cit.*

extreme. The limelight of his youth was gone but he certainly never became the proverbial 'neglected artist' without fame or funds: to the last he was receiving commissions and on his death his estate came to a comfortable £1,500.

His last hours were spent in the company of Edward Burne-Jones. A brief account of their meeting survives in Georgiana Burne-Jones's *Memorials:* "December 10th [1883] is fixed in my mind because I was in town that evening and in returning home called by appointment for Edward at the Athenaeum. There he and Mr Doyle had met accidentally, and joining each other at the same table had spent a pleasant time together till Edward went up to the library. On coming down again about half past nine, he told me, he saw a knot of men clustered round something in the hall, and going nearer he found there his companion of an hour ago lying already unconscious, from the seizure which preceded his death".[20] Richard died the following morning without regaining consciousness. He was 59. Of his lifetime's work virtually the only part unknown to the public was the journal that follows.[21]

20. Georgiana Burne-Jones, *Memorials of Edward Burne-Jones* (2 vols., 1904), II, p. 138.
21. A cross-section of Richard Doyle's work can be seen most conveniently in Daria Hambourg's *Richard Doyle* (1948); the book has a useful introduction and a full list of his works.

A NOTE ON THE *JOURNAL*
AND THIS EDITION

During his lifetime Richard Doyle kept the *Journal* very much to himself; even Holman Hunt, an old and close friend, did not see it. But the obscurity did not last: less than two years after his death a facsimile was published by Smith, Elder and Company, with an introduction by J. H. Pollen. And in the same year, 1885, Richard's sister Annette sold the original to the British Museum, for the considerable sum of £200; there it remains, in the care of the Department of Prints and Drawings.

Sadly, this facsimile does less than justice to the delicacy of Richard's penmanship. Over the years the writing and sketches of the original, done in Chinese ink with a quill pen, have faded and the paper has yellowed, to the point where a satisfactory reproduction by conventional printing methods has become impossible. So this edition has to be a reproduction of the 1885 facsimile, itself not a particularly sensitive rendering. The spirit of the original *Journal* is in these pages, but not, alas, the full quality.

The Smith, Elder editor decided in a few places to add words or letters, in a matching writing style, where Richard had nodded ("wreaths", line 16, p. 21 is an example); and pages left blank in the original were silently elided. No other changes were made. Some sketches in the original are roughly pencilled but not completely or at all inked in: where this occurs an indication is given in the 'Notes', since the pencil is too faint to print.

A JOURNAL

BY

DICK DOYLE

1840

Illustrated with ... hundred ...

By the AUTHOR

1841 January

DICK DOYLES JOURNAL

JANUARY

WEDNESDAY. The first of January. Got up late, very bad. Made good resolutions and did not keep them. Went out and got a cold. Did keep it. First thought I would, then thought I would not, was sure I would, was positive I would not, at last was determined I would, write a journal. Began it. This is it and I began it on the first of January, one thousand eight hundred and forty. Hope I may be skinned alive by wild cats if I dont go on with it

Thursday 2. One oclock. went to the park though I have a cold with a boy named Henry and a little dog called Puff. Saw a party of artillery jetting powder at the magazine, and thought a great many wise thing about powder magazines taking fire and blowing quantities of unfortunate little men up into the air. Then the boy the dog and I had a curious running game up and down the Serpentine, and returned home in safty I am afraid this journal will turn out a hash. Good bye

Tuesday 3. Up at eight, out at one, home at three, dinner at four tea at seven, bed at eight, cold very bad, took pints of barley water

1

going to bed and could not write my journal till to day because I was afraid of staying up in the cold, what a sensible boy I must be to be sure The barley water did not do any good and I roared coughing all night. Of course I excited a great deal of pity next morning. I could not help it, Now what do you think I will just do, why if it does not get better before to night I wont go to bed at all. for I would much sooner cough three hours by day than one by night

Saturday 4th Up late, lazy, cant help, cold bad Great excitement. John Frost and co who are about to be tried for high treason at Monmouth I dont know much of what is going on at present because I could not get a look at the paper all the week. At all events I will have a good read of the "Observer to morrow and then I can see " The whole of the full and true account "

Sunday 5th Could not go out so I amused myself till ten with coffee and bread and butter. The show being over I suddenly seised the idea by the collar, and rushed up stairs to begin a little regiment of musicians with big heads, on a strip of paper, height. one inch. I intend giving them to papa when finished. six are done. Papa and James have walked to Hendon, or some such place. it is very cold, I want to go out. I cant. and here I sit.

Monday 6th Cough a leetle better. Went to the park for two hours. and then slipped into Piccadilly for the purpose of seeing the first number of the new historical romance by W H Ainsworth called" The Tower of London embellished with three steel engravings and wood cuts by George Cruikshank in each part price one shilling. the first number of Guy Fawkes by the same, and of Poor Jack by Captain Marryat illustrated by Stan. field I came home at five thinking the whole way what would be the name of

Bos's new work to begin on the first of March. I did some of the little musicians, then took my dinner, then took my tea then took my supper and then
took myself to bed

Tuesday 7th I am beginning to suspect that my cold is not much better for going out
yesterday, as I coughed nearly all night, besides keeping up a smart battery of those
curious noises most of the day. Uncle brought in" The Tower of London" at dinner
and I hearing that it was soon going to be read aloud, escaped up stairs by the
back door, came down again before it was finished and (it not being worth while to
go up again) was obliged to hear the end of the second chapter, where the Duke of
Northumberland forces the earls of Arundel Burliegh and others, to sign their
names to an answer to a letter from the princess Mary wherein she claims
the allegiance of the aforesaid earls. I should say in the words of fat Dr Johnson,
that the passage deserves praise and merits commendation".

Wednesday 8th Very frosty. Did some of the little musicians with big heads
and nearly finished them, after which I had a glorious read of the paper including the whole of the Attorney Generals speech on the opening of Frosts trial, but
here is Uncle just come into the room with Bentley in his hand and as every
one but myself are just going to dinner I should not be surprised if I got first
read of Guy Fawkes.

Thursday 9th I dont much like the opening of Guy Fawkes but I suppose it
will turn out something very interesting indeed.
There is a new story by the author of Valentine Vox
but who he is, perhaps Jupiter knows. I dont.
I have seen the paper to day but there is nothing important therein, I am meditating a
Quenten Durward on a sheet of double elephant

3

but I must get the Tournament finished before I begin any thing else as there is some chance of its being published; if it does, that day will be a very extraordinary one in my life. The sketches are nearly finished.

Friday 10th. Got up early and finished all the little musicians with big heads all but one nose. I was just going to begin the "History of Belgium" when I found the paper all wet. It is suspected to be the work of an incendiary. What an unfortunate circumstance to be sure.

Saturday 11th. This morning I did Mr Jerningham on a horse and Pratt on a ladder by which extraordinary feat I rendered the sketches for the Tournament finished. Aunt Anne gave me a little life of Mary Queen of Scots by A Cunningham, which I have been reading these few days. It is about the most minute history I ever read, and places the character of Mary in a very favorable light. The Tournaments are all finished but the title page and I expect to have it done next week, and then "Hurra"   Dont you be too sure though, perhaps they wont be published at all.

Sunday 12th. Not been out yet, what a nice business. This is Sunday morning and I have nothing to show. I always show Papa whatever I have done in the week and if I had nothing else I would show such a thing as this.

Now it appears that I have not done a sufficient quantity of work in past week and therefore deserve one or more moderately good kicks.

Monday. I feel impressed with a belief that I will never see the Tourney in print but who knows whether I wont see myself in a shop window one of these fine no not fine but horribly rainy mornings At all events it wont break my leg if I just finish them. I was up early. Good boy. I really begin to suspect I am getting better I do and besides that I think the Frosts trial will be finished to morrow. Now just imagine if I was. was walking along coolly, and suddenly came upon the Tournament in a shop window. Oh crikey it would be enough to turn me inside out

Wedesday. After breakfast, wished the paper would come till it did. Frost con- demned. Read the life of Mary Queen of Scots, till I came to the murder of Riz- zio. bye the bye a new play called Mary Stuart will be brought out at Drury Lane in a few days, the part of Ruthven M? Macready. It is an interesting subject for a play but Papa says the name is calculated to make people expect too much. I worked away at exercises till bedtime and then I went.

Thursday. The paper is putting into its columns interesting little anecdotes about Prince Albert. For instance it appeared this morning. that the Queen and her intended, when children were much together, learnt their tiny tasks together." oh goodness" and often from the very same identical little interesting volume "oh my" what shall I do it is so very ---- I dont know what. M? Street came at one and went at three. At the present moment I am horribly disgusted with this journal, principally on account of the frightful productions which embellish the opposite page, now there are a great number of ladies and gentlemen who labouring under the same feelings of disapprobation would say good afternoon to it at once, but I (wise youth) am determined to go on.

FRIDAY. Oh so the Queen *is* going to be married to Prince Albert is she, very well dont cry. Who is prince Albert, why dont you know. he is the youngest son of the duke of Saxe Coberg and Gotha, wonderful, what an extraordinary fact. Just as if I did not know that" Well if you did what did you ask one for" Because I liked" more stupid you" mind your own business" Wont" Well then dont kick up such a row about nothing.

Saturday If ever living creatures feelings received a severe shock, those feelings were mine at half past eleven this morning, when a report was spread that we were again to visit Harbours, for the purpose of learning that very revolting species of amusement, the dance. There exists in Oxford Terrace a man, one James Harbour, who teaches this thing. James Harbour is a specimen of animated nature of rather tall proportions, with falling shoulders, a powerful pair of legs and a peculiarly bitter smile. He performs a few characteristic airs on the violin. This mans powers are very extraordinary, he has been known to put out a candle, on a high table

with his foot, it the foot, being at the time, cased in a striped silk stocking and a patent pump. The severe shock sustained by my feelings at this in-telligence must be left to the imagination.

The little sketch on the opposite page will give some idea of the manner in which the establishment is conducted. Lord Alfred Paget has gone to Germany to bring over the happy man. Mr Steel came at twelve and I did a considerable quantity of the Tournament.

SUNDAY My cold is in a high state of preservation; now really it is a great annoyance that I cant go out. Today was so fine and there was I pent up in the house like a a---a I dont remember exactly what I was like, but it was something very horrible I am sure. I translated some history of Belgium.

Monday. Very hard frost and I cant go out. dreadful. I hardly know what to do, and to make it worse theres a man just gone by with a pair of skates and a red nose. A great many curious feats are per-formed on the ice for instance the winter before last, in the Regents Park at about a quarter to three I fell down on my nose just like this and got up in a state of excruciating torture. I consoled myself with this pleasant reminiscence and drew till dinner, after which satisfactory ceremony I wrote a page of all my exercises I am so sick with this book that I wont let any one see it at least for a year. quite horrid, good bye.

7

Tuesday 20th More frost. Mr Street came at half past twelve and went at two. Theres a great chance of Frosts getting off altogether for this reason that according to the law no prisoner should be punished with a copy of the indictment and a list of the witnesses ten days before trial, now one of the lists was delivered ten days before but the other was given thirteen days before, so that if anything, it was an advantage to the prisoner yet for this reason the man is likely to be let off. The case is to be decided by the fifteen judges at Westminster. Now there is something very pleasant about all this, high treason, why it is quite delightful, so historical, and it must be more particularly gratifying &c to Prince Albert, who is coming very shortly

Wednesday 20th The fringe for the Queens wedding dress has cost three hundred pounds. The wedding itself is to take place at eight oclock on the 12th of February in St James chapel. It is said prince Albert wont arrive till the day before at all events I intend seeing both on the day though I get crushed to death in the attempt. James has been to Grass and got a sheet of transfer so I am regularly in for it "hura". I never knew anything equal to it since my existence in this civilized world

Thursday 22d I am working away at the Tournament like I dont know what. I have spoiled two ("hura") and have begun a third which, if it succeed will be marched off to Grass tomorrow morning, and really I hope it may for I have had trouble enough though of course I dont mind that "hura" I am moreover in such a state of excitement that I can hardly sit in my shoes "Hurra"

8

Friday 23° Really the idea of one of my delectable works going off to a printers wrapped up in light brown paper placed in a portfolio of one foot nine by thirteen inches is rather too much for my senses, so I was not up too early but lay awake thinking what sort of thing it would look like. I had a strong conviction that it would appear rather like a great number of lines running and twisting all over the paper representing men armour and horses &.. mixed up with horrible quantities of rain and blots, and so it turned out for I was looking out of the window when suddenly I nearly fell out. and James was seen walking up the Terrace. There was the identical drawing in a most awful state almost all the lines had swelled and it was blotted beautifully but as I know the reason I wont give in but will just begin another this evening and have it finished early tomorrow morning The truth of the business is that the paper got greasy and that together with the ink being put on too thickly, produced the uncommonly agreeable affect before alluded to. I was under the impression that the ink must must be put on very thick to make it print at all but in reality the thinner the better.

SATURDAY 24 Hurra! printed gloriously "hurra!" I will have another done tomorrow hurra! The running at the dummy hurra!" Get them all done in three weeks hurra Dont think I will sleep to night "Hurra!"

9

SUNDAY 25. Up at eight. Went to the park at one. Could not keep from the Tournament even to day so I began "The procession to the lists"

MONDAY 26th I could not get "The Procession" finished to day in time to go. more the pity. Never mind no damage done I think I will do The Tilt next. The Queens marriage is drawing near and if I am to believe everything I read thirteen English noblemen have gone to Germany to give Prince Albert the order of the Garter among others Lords Alfred and Clarence Paget, Viscount Torrington Col Grey &c

TUESDAY 27th James went to Grass with the "Procession" at twelve, and as I could not do anything till I saw how it looked. I rushed into the park in a frantic manner, to make the time pass. I saw the last number of Michael Armstrong, got unwell at the sight of one of the illustrations. Mr Roney came and gave us a ticket for the Polytecnic, and James came home with the "Tilt". Printed very well. Four done out of six. "Hurra" !.

WEDNESDAY 29th. "Spoiled" go on, no use talking about it now it is done Must begin it again. may as well do it at once, did. got a head ache galloped into the park, trotted round it, came home. head all gone; I dont like to begin anything till these are finished but most assuredly as soon as they are, I will begin a large picture of the feast of the Scottish Archers from Quinten Durward on a sheet of double elephant. Papa thinks I aught, I think I aught and I dont care a button hole who thinks

I aught not. I made considerable progress in the "Tilt" this evening.

Thursday. 30th First preparing for and then with McStreet till two o'clock. I fin-ished the Tilt by four; James took it to the printers after dinner. I am partic-ularly anxious to see this one done because it will try the powers of transfer more than any one I have done yet, from the number of little heads in the back-ground though perhaps not more than the second of "The running at the Quenton". I find that there is nothing like putting the ink on the pen thin.

Friday 31st. Was out most of the morning. James went for the "thing" at one but they said it would not be done till five. I could not do any more to day. I felt so tired and sick of the feeling of drawing on transfer paper I suppose it will go off tomorrow. it nearly did to night when I saw the "Tilt" brought in, it had printed so well

FEBRUARY.

SATURDAY. Oh this is the first of February is it. Well and what of it. Only just that I was nearly forgetting it and just going on without putting the new month in large letters at the top, but fortunately I did not, most likely because I did not know that there was thirty two days in January. I worked hard at the Tournament most of the day but I am afraid I must take a rest for a day or two. because after drawing much on transfer paper. I get sick of the feeling it.

11

SUNDAY. Went to chapel at eight after breakfast went with Henry to see the Queen return from church. Although there were not more than a hundred persons there altogether owing to the badness of the weather, a middle aged man of respectable appearance in his anxiety, lest he should not obtain a view of his beloved sovereign, clung to a lamp post with desperate eagerness resolved to see his Queen or perish in the attempt. There was not the slightest necessity for him to do the latter, for as I said before there were comparatively very few persons, there.

Monday   The intelligence this morning is as important and curious as it is interesting, namely that Mrs Gunter and Waud the confectioners have been commanded to supply her Majesty with a great beast of a plum cake, some ten feet in circumference, to be followed up by a hundred others of a more decent size, which are to be distributed among her majesty's friends. A portrait from life of the interesting big un has appeared in all the printshop windows

Tuesday. I was passing down Bond Street this afternoon and was not a little

surprised at seeing something which without the aid of a telescope looked horribly like a party of offensive individuals waylaying the house of a respectable confectioner, and carrying the door by storm. On enquiring the cause of so curious a proceeding I learnt that the anxious ladies and gentlemen were endeavouring to obtain a sight of the interesting great lump of cake which was on view within, and that as only one or two were allowed in at a time and the ladies and gentlemen being as I before hinted, anxious, it required a strong built policeman to guide their motions He, the policeman was placed at the door, to hand the ladies and gentlemen in and out, and I having nearly burst myself in an ineffectual attempt to break in, walked away thinking.

Wednesday What a funny man Braham is, the only time I ever saw Braham was, one night last year, in the opera of Massanello at the St James's theatre, when just at the beginning of the second act, when the audience were glowing with delight at the beautiful chorus of fishermen, suddenly, quite suddenly a little fat man with a red cloak thrown gracefully over his left shoulder and a great bare neck covered with whiskers rushed in, and darting down to the front of the stage, and stretching

13

out, with one hand on his heart and the other in the air, as far as he possibly could without falling into the pit, burst out in a loud voice "Behold how brightly breaks the morning" whereupon the whole house stood up and cheered. While the ruffian of the piece, a six foot fisherman stood by with his hand on a great carving knife and his legs stamping about the stage in a frantic manner. I was quite charmed, so was the house. The same ruffian who was really one Howell in disguise, at a later period of the evening tried to sing a song, which he did in such an abominable style, that the house hissed, all but two respectable gentleman, who being in the gallery, wore their hats, and gloried in it, and who, not because they thought the thing either good or bad but in opposition to the rest of the house set up a feeble cheer (this encouraged the poor ruffian who was evidently on the point of crying) the house only hissed more, and he finished amidst a running accompaniment of hisses and feeble cheers. It was during this memorable evening, that the following incident occurred which proves in a strong light what a deceptive machine a hat is. While we were waiting for the Ballet uncle descried Sheriden Knowles in a box opposite, and left me to go to him.

Impelled by a desire to view this individual closely. I darted into a neighbouring hat, (which I conceived uncle had left) and drew forth from its depths an opera glass and forthwith began to scrutinize the features of the illustrious poet, while in the act of doing which I was alarmed by hearing a voice in my ear demand in a soft tone who gave me leave to use that glass. I immediately shook. first looked at the glass. then in the direction of the voice and oh frightful there was a man. The glass was a strange glass. with an ivory handle, the man was a little man with one leg up on the seat. I explained. he smiled. I begged his pardon, he begged mine. I endeavoured to replace the instrument, he requested I would not, I did. he took it out again and said that I would greatly oblige him by using it again. I did "Then he said" were you ever in this theatre before" and I said" no" "Nice little theatre" and I said" yes". This remarkable occurence took place at about eleven oclock. The man was a tight little gentleman of about five feet one in pointed boots with a beautiful color. in his face and charming little whiskers on his head and a benignant smile on his mouth He was altogether what would be termed a tight little gentlemen, of about five and twenty summers

Saturday. Mr Strees came at one and went at two. after which I went to the park but recollecting that Prince Albert was to arrive at the Clarendon this afternoon. I went, but though I saw a great crowd. I could not see him, and as I can see a crowd whenever I take the

15

trouble to walk into Oxford street I did not wait, and as it was time for dinner I came home and heard that most likely he would arrive at the palace first. The first night of Leigh Hunts play." The Legend of Florence.

Sunday. Chapel at eight. breakfast nine. Went to see prince Albert go to church, did not see him because he did not go. pity. see what I can do tomorrow. It is a great bore that the "Observer" has not been got to day because then perhaps I might see a list of the Procession tomorrow. I think I will make an effort to see the man.

Monday. The long expected day at length arrived in pouring rain and I stood looking out of the parlor window till half past eleven. It would have been better to have done something for besides making the time pass quicker, then would not have been any time lost, but I am one of those interesting kind of individuals, who whenever they have once worked themselves up into the idea of seeing any very extraordinary object of art or animated nature, can not possibly set to work at any kind of business whatsoever; until the said objects of art or animated nature have been duly witnessed, and so it was this day. Dispair was in my face at half past eleven. but it passed away at twelve. for the rain ceasing. and the sky brightning a little. I thought the opportunity was not to be lost. as it might begin to rain again. so together with Henry who was in the same state as myself we

16

sallied in company with an umbrella which was rayther the worse for the wear, and reached the scene of action S.ᵗ James Park, just in time to behold the tops of six carriages with the tops of half a dozen footmen hanging at the backs, and twenty times that number of tops of life guardsmen

This view was so pleasant and gratifying that it was a wonder we did not go home quite satisfied, or else take our station in the same place to see the return, but we (just like us) were not satisfied and wished to get a nearer view, so that when the hour of return arrived we fought with the desperate determination of seeing the happy couple or of returning home without obtaining a sight of them. I am a boy of about fifteen years of age, measuring something like five feet in height and endowed with such prodigeous strength as to be capable of knocking a little man down in a crowd. My brother Henry is equaly wonderfull for personal strength having been known to knock three boys down an area at one burst. With such power as there we plunged into the crowd without fear. In the first place a life Guardsman began to make his horse kick and plunge in a most awful manner frightening all the respectable persons within thirty yards of him, out of their senses. Then came the police pushing and thumping in such a violent way, that Henry and I

were on the point of death from suffocation. However after half an hours tremendous bodily exertion, our efforts were crowned with success and we found ourselves in undisturbed possession of places in the front row, with no other inconvenience than that arising from the momentarily expectation of a bushel of men and boys falling on our heads, and the commotion which usually succeeds the words "Farther back here" accompanied by the application of policemans shoulders against the chests of unoffending people whereby very nearly terminating their existence by premature suffocation the said policeman who behaves in this benevolent manner will talk in the most friendly manner possible the while, for instance he will say. "I dont want to hurt you, you know" and then make a most desperate lunge at a mans head "I must do my duty" at the same time throwing himself against me with frightful violence, then a little funny old cobler who is nearly bursting with kindness. because he has a good place himself, says. "Of course he must why dont you keep back there".

It is remarkable how good humoured crowds are on these occasions, all except the old women with coal scuttle bonnets and green umbrellas, and they are fearful. A footman who stood next to me was a nice specimen of that cheerfulness which is so refreshing to meet in society. his wit and lively conversation were not to be withstood. Suddenly the guns which were to announce the ceremony over. began to fire and a loud shout followed. rain poured down and umbrellas were put up, policemen feeble with their exertions thrust their staffs under their arms and for the first time stood still. The crowd for want of something better to do roared laughing whenever anyone fell out of a tree, or screamed hooting whenever a dog appeared on the road. The day began to clear up a little at about half past one. the day began to look smiling. The false alarms were innumerable. Every minute there was a cry of "Here she is" Every neck was stretched out to its utmost with expectation. A footman next me said he wished if she was coming at all she would make haste, which sagacious remark unfortunately produced no effect. A little blackguard boy climbed nimbly up to the top of a tree, and shouted out "Hoora" and having given way to this remarkable sentiment climbed down again. It was then that two Life Guards and a loud scream announced the return of the happy pair which was followed by carriages containing the following. distinguished individuals. In the first were. the duke of Saxe Coburg, prince Ernest and two gentlemen in waiting on their royal highnesses, in the second were two maids of honor and an equerry, the third, the lord

20

chamberlain and three pages of honor in the fourth lord Hill and some other gentlemen whom I had not the honor of knowing the fifth, the earl of Almermale and the Duchess of Sutherland, in the sixth, the Queen and Prince Albert. The cheers were tremendous and Henry and I waved our hats and screamed with all our might The Queen was on the opposite side of the coach. but we saw prince Albert as well as could be, he was dressed in the costume of Field Marshal with the order of the Garter round his neck and a large white satin bow on each shoulder. he looked very handsome, and the Queen with a large viel over her head, looked actually beautiful. The duke of Sussex followed, and I must not forget to add eight bridesmaids whom we saw very well owing to the stoppage of the carriages by the crowd. At four oclock after partaking of a splendid break- fast the Queen and Prince Albert went to Windsor, carriages and people lining the whole way for miles. and the line as far as Hamersmith decorated with flowers and illuminations wreaths of laurel and flags innumerable. and lastly a triumphal arch at Kensington. I returned home very tired. ate beef and drank the mans health, went up the Edgware road to see lord Sureys illu- minations, no great things. came back again, horribly tired, put myself on one chair and my feet on another and began to read "The confessions of Harry Lorriquer"

Tuesday. As soon as Mr Street went, I went, I went for the first time to Graff I began to feel seriously alarmed when I neared the fatal house. I went in. nothing dreadful took place.

scraped out on the stone, whatever I wanted. saw Count D'Orsay who came to see one of his portraits on the stone. Came home at five

Tuesday 8th As might have been expected I was not up too soon. and though I knew it was past eight I would persuade my-  self that it was not nearly seven yet. At last after tremendous ex- ertion both of body and mind. I contrived to sit up in the bed, by degrees I dragged myself towards the edge of the machene. and suddenly fell out on the floor. This curious evolution quickly brought me to a state of sensibility. and recollecting that, that desirable cere- -mony*was not to be got though without making down the stairs, and as it would not be considered proper to make down stairs in a night shirt, particularly as the weather was rather icy; you may judge that I was not slow in dressing. I did some of the Tourna- ment Mc.Steet came and went, the paper came and went too with- out me seeing it, but uncle bought it in the evening so I read the

* breakfast

whole account. Some of the illuminations were on a grand scale
for instance The Royal Academy, the duke of Devonshires, the Club
houses &c. I shall never forget the night the Queen became of age,
when we all went out to see the illuminations. The crowd was by
far the most tremendous thing I ever experienced; we were quite
an hour going along Pall Mall, and sometimes we could not move
a foot for ten minutes. At the corner of S.t James's Street it was ter-

-riffic, the two crowds meeting. While the women were screaming
the men were cursing and kicking. One great fat man began to
throw himself against the people for his amusement, while another
said to a country looking man who had a little infant on his head,
D——m you what have you brought the child into the crowd to kill
it for, whereupon the countryman says, Mind your business and leave

me to mind mine," at the same time as an old woman says," Well Louisa never say you were not in a crowd after this" and Louisa assures her that she never will. There was a grand banquet at S.t James's palace yesterday evening at which were all the household, and the ministers all gave dinner parties

Wednesday. When I was at this day in the scribble I either forgot or purposely did not write anything so that I will draw a little man instead.

Thursday. I worked away at the Tournament like shot from a gun. James goes to Graf every day either to get me one proofed or to get a pen. The Queen is coming to town on Saturday

Friday. Talk of coincidences the most extraordinary one I ever knew was that the duke of Wellington, Napoleon and Mahomet Ali were all born in the same year. Shakespere died on his birth day, Charles the 11.d made his entry into London after the Restoration on his

Saturday. Henry and I went to the park to day and chancing to pass Hyde Park corner saw a crowd of people standing in evedens expectation of some person or thing, then it was that it occurred to me that the Queen was coming to town" Suppose we stop says I "Letts says Henry" and we did. The people began gradually to collect on Constitution Hill from 12 o'clock upwards. It was horribly cold and to make it worse we had Ruff with us. The crowd was very great and the chairs tables and benches were nearly as numerous as on the marriage day. Expectation being at the highest, at five minutes past four, six light dragoons galloped up and took their stations on each side of the Triumphal arch, a few minutes more and the cortege appeared in sight tearing down Constitution hill at most tremendous pace "now for it," "heres a go," what is to be done with Ruff, "tremendous rush" oh lad" Henry seized her up and rushed towards the arch the dog the while giving vent to a series of remarkable howls, that was all I saw. I had enough to do take care of myself.

The carriages drove bye I saw the Queen very well but Prince Albert was on the other side. After some difficulty I found Henry out, and having ascertained that the dogs bones were whole, we made haste home.

Wednesday. I meant to have gone to Grass to day, but at twelve oclock much to the surprise of the inhabitants of this house it began to snow heavily and continued to do so the greater part of the day. I began the History of Belgium to day and did a page and a half. I hope I wont spoil it and so have to begin it a third time. I am not quite sure about the title "The History of Belgium" wont do because it is only a part of it as it begins at the year 14 hundred or thereabouts, so that I must call it "The History of Belgium" from such a year to such a year. I dont expect the Tournament to be out for a week at least. The duke of Wellington is recovering fast from his late illness

Thursday 20th Mr Street came at two. it snowed last night and is very cold to day Did two pages of Belgium History, and used the dumb bells to an enormous extent and finished one of my Quentin Durwards, and a "Tournament"

Trsday. Up at eight. hard frost. Went out before breakfast to see if the ice was strong enough to bear, it was not so I came home and after breakfast did The History of Belgium for two hours. Went out again, came home half dead, horrible cold, dreadful easterly wind, walked into the fire and got restored. James went to Mr Westall to ask him what sort of a man Tilt the publisher was. Mr Westall said he was Jewish and wanted fifty per cent while Ackerman whom he recommended, only forty

MONDAY. nothing came to day except Mr Steel and Mr More O Ianel.

Tuesday. At a meeting held in Exeter no Freemasons hall, some respectable gentlemen took it into their heads to create an uproar and upset the tables and benches and Mr Hume whereby producing on the part of that gentleman great bodily fear and a strong desire to evacuate the premises, which he did accordingly with remarkable swiftness The day is very cold and I went out to get colder so that I might enjoy my feed. I am going to bed in a minute

SUNDAY. Cold. frosty home breakfast hot. out. back again. dinner. Now as I done "The Tournament" I must begin to have shows again on Sundays I must indeed. Its shocking. The Penny Magazine for this week has a continuation

27

of the life of Mr John Elwes the miser in it and as the following little
anecdote from it might be worth remembering for the purpose of showing
what a sublime being an apothecary is. I will put it down
"Mr Elwes returning home from the house one night unforti-
nately came in contact with a sedan chair which cut his legs severely. He was
carried into a friends house, which was close bye. At first he would not
allow a surgeon to be sent for, but after repeated entreaties he suffered an
apothecary to be called, who when he arrived of course began to make long
faces and speeches about the badness of the case. Come said Elwes you take
one leg and will take the other and see which will be well first. Do what
ever you like to yours, and I will do nothing to mine. The man agreed
and Mr Elwes got his well first by a fortnight. His uncle who was just such
another as himself, had his house broken into by robbers who after first bind
ing his only man servant in the stable ran up stairs to the bed room
of the miser and presenting their pistols at him swore to shoot him
if he did not immediately give up his money. He at first showed them

a draw in which was 70" pounds, but the men knew that he had more and again threatened him, when at last he gave them five thousand or something of that sort which the villains carried off and which the Penny Magazine says was one of the greatest money robberies ever committed. They left him saying that one of the party would remain below to to murder him if he attempted to call for assistance. Mr Elwes said I give you twenty minutes to escape after that time nothing shall prevent one from going to see what has become of my servant. When Mr Elwes died the only one who shed a tear for him was the same servant man.

MARCH

SUNDAY Went to chapel at 8. after breakfast showed papa the first number of the History of Belgium and he liked it. Mr F Selous came this morning at about 11 oclock. I could not go out so I tried a little more Belgium, and so on till dinner, though I know that it is not at all proper to do any thing of that sort on Sundays but I can not read for more than an hour at a time so that I must either do it or nothing at all. Mr Rothwell came in the evening and Papa asked him to come to the Polytechnic Institution to morrow evening with us. and he said that he would.   amen

29

Monday. Heres a game. James asked at Graf's how soon the copies would be printed and they said tomorow. I can hardly do anything till I see them. It turned out that the pol- etecnec is not open now in the evening so that we wont go. What a pity.

Tuesday. Uncomfortable thing. I am afraid that Mr Street will come before the "Tournament" so that when The Tournament would come Mr Street would be here. There was no fear however for at 12 oclock fifty hot copies arrived per Graf's man. I never knew such fun in my whole life. I gave Mr Street one and every half hour in the day ran to look at them to see if I could find out anything new. Annette has gone to the opera this the first night, Torquato Tassa; oh my goodness me fifty hot pressed copies of the Tournament I wont beleive it. "Hurrä

Thursday. no Wedessday. As soon as I got up this morning I ran to have a look at the fifty copies to see how they looked on the second day of arrival. Of course they looked beautiful I began the illustrations to the History of Belgium to day but some how or other I could not work. I suppose that the publication has acted so powerfully on my system, that I am not able to anything. It is a wonder I was able to eat any dinner. Uncle has got an interesting book by Lodge of a collections of facsimilies of letters of illustrious persons from Henry the eight upwards they are very numerous. so I have chosen a few of the most interesting autographs as I think they are interesting.

30

They are those of Mary Queen of Scots. Henry son of James the first, Wolsey,
Oliver Cromwell. Sir Thomas Moore and Cramer

MAY H R Oliver Cromwell

Thomas Cantuaryi Henry

Tho Moor. T Car hs Cooz

Dick Doyle.

Thursday. Oh my, late, make haste up, make haste down, breakfast. Pity it was not all gone. I went to the park with Ruff. and after
dinner Papa gave me the money to buy a sheet of double elephant
to begin my large Quentin Durward on, which I intend if possible
to do tomorow.

FRIDAY 6 After a little deliberation. I went to Ackermans
to get the double elephant. I pasted it down on a large canvas as
soon as I came home
and it went on well
I spent the rest of the -
day in thinking how
glorious it would be
beginning it tomorow
morning." Hurra "

31

SATURDAY I went to the Serpentine this morning and to my great astonishment found that the ice bore very well, of course I took advantage of so pleasant and unusual a circumstance and performed curious feats on it for more than an hour.

Sunday. Have I anything to show. No. with the exception of a sheet of double elepant. I have nothing. At two oclock I went with Annette to Mr Selous and came home by five. It is quite extraordinary to think of there being ice all over the serpentine on such a burning hot day as this

Monday. Glorious fun. Papa said he would put James into oil colors to day so accordingly he set to at copying Mr Rothwells Adelaide. More fun we have taken our things out into the large room, and I have began my Quinten Durward and have working hard all day on it. Wonderful

appetite mime after working hard all day on a Quentin Durward four feet some inches by two feet some more inches. on an easel.

Tuesday. Fine day. did my exercises &c. till two. and Quenten all the rest of the day except when I went out. I must begin coloring it tomorrow.

WEDNESDAY I strongly suspected when I got up this morning, that I had a cold in my head in event of which suspicion turning out true. there would be every reason to suppose it caused by a sudden change which took place in the weather yesterday. It did not however prevent me from going out so I went to the

palace yard. It was very cold and showers of hail paid frequent visits to the metropolis during the day. When I came home I found a pretty kettle of fish

no vandyke brown. Cant go on with my picture. Oh my at about 2 o'clock Graf had the villainy to send his bill and I have not yet got a farthing so that I suppose that after all I shall go to jail. what a pity.

The Queen commanded Charles Kemble to play "Felix in the "Wonder", last night and she and prince Albert honored the Theatre with their presence. There was a great cry for God save the Queen, and Mr Bartley came forward and said that although they were not prepar-

33

-ed they would do their best so accordingly they did after the play On coming from her box her Majesty sent for Mr Kemble and compli mented him on his performance. He is to play Mercutio tomorrow.

THURSDAY. When I awoke this morning I felt so unwell that I thought I was going to be laid up but I felt certain that I was lying down which rendered the circumstance re-markable. However as I began to get wider awake and more sensible I could not help thinking that after all there was nothing very dreadful the matter only the head ache and sickness which usualy accompanies a cold in the head. and what would be the use of staying in bed for it so after a desperate combat with my inclinations in which I fought under great disadvantage, (as I was lying down) I dashed up and rushed down stairs, no not dashed, but walked with a solemn kind of silly expression, to breakfast "Goodness" at twelve Grafs man came to be paid. the brute

I would just like to know what he wants money for. and he was paid, of course he was and I have only sold two copies. one to Aunt Anne and one to Mr Mone, and the bill is four pound eighteen. It is a nice

34

business to say the truth. and now it is worse than it was before for there is something pleasant and important in paying a printers bill, but nothing in paying a debt to Papa which I will have to do now. But supposing I don't get any more sold, then what will I do.

Friday. To day is the anniversary of the birth day of Prince George of Cambridge and after a grand dinner party. the whole set went to the Haymarket to see Power on "his last legs" by particular desire Uncle has been all day out so I suppose he has gone there too.

MONDAY. Went to the palace yard again to day. Really I am quite musical. that is three times I have gone this week. At all events

it is well worth the walk there. They play beautifully and the best compositions besides. For my part I would not complain if I never heard a better band. I look forward to next Sunday  with much interest on account of a certain enormous bet made between Papa and I. viz that I would not get a second number of 'The History of Belgium' done against the Sunday following the first of April. Papa bet half a crown that I would not, I bet a shilling that I would. Now as this is a very serious affair I am in a considerable state of mental excitement and look forward to the appointed day with a mixture of mingled hope and fear.

Tuesday. Mr Street went at two. I worked on Quentin till two. rain rain, rain.

WEDNESDAY.

I went to the palace yard They played a beautiful air air from Tor- quato Tasso. The Tower of London is out for April Great interest

Here is a pretty piece of business. This mornings paper said that there would be a drawing room to day and under that impression Henry and I stayed out till two waiting to see the Queen going to S'. James's Palace, and then after waiting all that time (that is from a quarter to eleven) a sentinel told us that there would be none to day. In the evening Mr Rothwell came with a bit of intelligence, peculiarly agreeable to my private feelings, in other words Mr Rothwell was at a party last night at Mrs Franklin Lewis's where he showed the "Tournament" and the consequence was that a lady wished to get it and so the next morning she came to Mr Rothwell to know if the thing was to be got anywhere and Mr R recollecting that he knew a person who did the thing and who could perhaps furnish the information desired came here this evening and has only just gone taking with him one copy for the aforesaid lady.

Thursday. "More fun" took two copies to "Mr Chorley." hurra. Mr Rothwell came in with seven and six and said he wanted another copy for a friend of Mr Franklin Lewis. Glorious." Now perhaps I have a chance of being able to pay the bill, I took the copy for Mrs Franklin Lewis's friend this afternoon.

FRIDAY

The Marquess of Landowne gave a grand ball last night at his house in Berkeley square at which were present the Queen and Prince Albert There was a bude light on a scaffolding in the middle of the garden which cast a brilliant light over the whole side of the square. Papa was passing at about eleven and he never saw anything of the kind to equal the number of carriages They reached from the house, round the square and then all the way down to Oxford Street. fresh ones were arriving every minute and as they were obliged to keep in two strings, some of the poor occupants had reason to suspect that they would not get in till morning. Master Humphreys clock struck one to day at six oclock with one illustration by Cattermole and two by Phiz. they are very nicely engraved, but there is no judging of the story as yet.

SATURDAY. As soon as Mr Street went I went to the park but had not farther than Victoria gate when suddenly I missed Ruff I first looked all about me and then darted home, she was not there, got a great fright and then darted out

again
in a
state
of agi-
tation
quite
indis-
cribable
and

who should I meet on the third Terrace from this but the identical little valuable trotting slowly towards home.

I am in a very critical state, working away at The History of Belgium which I must either have done by tomorrow morning or give Papa a shilling, so therefore I am working desperately, resolved not to go to bed till I have finished the illustrations. Humphreys Clock was read out 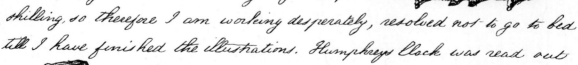 this evening and really I dont know what to make of it. **SUNDAY.** Well now this is all very pleasant. I have won half a crown. Papa liked the illustrations which was also pleasant. I walked in the park till dinner. Mr Selous came to tea "glorious" he took away half a dozen Tournaments to dispose of. Hurra Papa says that Mr O'Fanal showed it to lord Seymour.

Monday. James took one to Mr O'Connor and I went to see the people coming from the levee and after seeing the Queen and Prince Albert coming home to Buckingham Palace I went to the opera house to bring An- nette home from

a rehearsal, where after walking up and down for more than an hour I learnt that there had not been any to day in consequence of the band having to go to Hanover Square Rooms When I came home I heard the important intelligence that the Tournament had been shown to Count D'Orsay I never knew anything like it in my whole life

APRIL.

WEDNESDAY This being the day on which facetious persons are in the habit of making what are termed April fools, it reminds me of an anecdote which I dont think will be out of place if I relate "The Duke and Duchess of Lorraine being imprisoned by the French in the time of Louis XIV, planned their escape, which for some wise reason they determined to put into execution on the first of this month

When the morning arrived having disguised themselves as pesants they succeeded in escaping from their prison. They had not gone far when they were met by a man, who recognizing the duke, ran and informed the sentinel who being a deep sighted character only laughed and cried out "April fool" The man then told the guard, but they treated his story in the same way, with the exception of one man, who thought their might be some thing in it, at all events it was his duty to tell the Governor of the circum-stance, but that functionary burst out into a loud laugh and cried out "April fool" and here the story ends. History does not inform how soon the go-vernor found out his mistake, nor does it describe his expression when he did, but that is left to the imagin-ation. I do nothing all day but work-ing away on my big Quentin Durward

41

Thursday. Mr Rothwell came and paid me for one Tournament and brought the names of five more subscribers. Mr Harding amongst others. As soon as Mr Street went we set off for St James's Street to see the people going and coming from the Drawing Room. There was a great deal of merriment raised among the spectators by the frequent appearance

of couples of tall footmen stepping along the middle of the Street, which was dreadfully muddy, on their toes. their legs being clad in light pink silk stockings and they themselves being obliged to keep smiling blandly all the time although suffering extreme agonies of mind. The number of military men was also remarkable and in such varieties of uniform that you would hardly suppose their were so many different regiments, some walking all the way up St James's Street to get to their carriages with their hats in their hands while others stood at the door waiting till theirs came to them, but what was by far the best part of it was the carriages full of handsome ladies which kept pouring bye every minute. At half past three I rushed into the park and saw Prince Albert and the Queen going home to Buckingham Palace. I have a good mind to do a companion to the feast of the Scottish archers, from Quenten Durward, of Louis the XIᵗʰ and Charles the Bold, at the banquet.

42

Tuesday. Mr Mayne came this morning and gave James a lesson in fencing They played away at it for nearly an hour. It is great fun and the best thing in the world for making you warm.

Friday. Good hard work of Quenten Durward all day Mr Moore came in the evening and paid me for two copies of the "Tournament

SATURDAY. Nothing.

SUNDAY. Went to Chapel at eight home at nine. Mr Mayne came to breakfast and after that ceremony there was a show put forth in which their were some work of art of considerable merit. Those from the pencil of Masters Frank and Charles are particularly worthy of notice. A drawing made by the former smart gentleman is quite startling in point of effect. It is an original design from the History of England or rather of Scotland representing Prince Charles Edwards meeting with Cameron of Lochiel in the mountains. This production boldly conceived. beautifully treated and wonderfully executed is truly refreshing to behold. Such bursts of true genius are seldom met with.

MONDAY. This morning the sun was actually shining. and it was such a delightful sensation that I could not resist going out and so accordingly I went into the park and walked about for two hours making all sorts of resolutions about sketching from nature. this summer and autumn for I prefer autumn. decidedly.

43

TUESDAY.

THE OLD HAT.

Papa and Mr Mayne went down to Ealing this afternoon to take two beds in the "Old Hat" an Inn on the road about a mile beyond the town or village. Now you should know that their are two "old hats." The Original "Old Hat" and the "Old Hat and no mistake". The Original "Old Hat" is the "spurious Old Hat" being of the time of George the II but the "Old Hat and no mistake" is the genuine "Old Hat" being the cavaliers of the time of Charles the First. It is painted as large as life on the sign board which stands out on the opposite side of the road staring at the "Original" "Old Hat" which is about three doors off, as if it wondered how it could have the impudence to stand there. During the Civil war between Charles the First and the Parliament their was a battle foughts at Brentford between Prince Rupert and the Earl of Essex and Ealing was occupied by the Royalists although the battle was fought for the most part in the town of Brentford. Therefore it is not unlikely that the real Old Hat and no mistake might have had its origin in that event.

Wednesday.

Papa came home this morning at about ten and heard the

pleasing intelligence that Ruff has got four puppies. There is no seeing that sort of quadrupeds they will turn out, but there is one white one which looks pretty well. I wish I could get my Quentin finished

THURSDAY. I am just beginning to get up earlier in the mornings. for instance take this morning, half past five. Papa came home at ten. and at dinner told us the pleasing intelligence. that we were to go down to Ealing tomorrow by the half past eight oclock train. take a walk, then a lunch and then home.

Henry and I went with a copy of the Tournament to Mr Savage in Essex Street Strand. and when we were coming home passed Chapman and Halls and found that Humphreys Clock was just published

this evening instead of tomorrow, it being Good Friday. We went in and bought it. It was just six and all the men and boys from the booksellers were just rushing out with their bundles. The clock has got a good illustration by Cattermole and there is an interesting story in it. We must bring it to Papa tomorrow. I dare say he has not much to read at the "Old Hat

Friday. Fine day. breakfast quickly dispatched. set off at about twenty minutes to nine. Of all the beautiful sensations I ever felt, setting off by the Great Western railroad at nine in the morning, stands first

In the first place imagine the sun shining & making everything look yellow Then the numbers of coaches cabs and omnibusses the people together with the red lamps, hay and a great quantity, a kind of reddish sand, unite in producing one of the most pleasant.

appearances I ever beheld. We went into the room for paying and paid What an important thing that was, actually paying down ninepence each and taking up a piece of buff paper. then again in walking down a stone passage passage. and lastly in being stuffed into a carriage which was full already, by a conductor who was dreadfully cranky. After waiting about five minutes, during a gentle a man, who was walking up and down reading the newspaper, entertained the company with remarks on the infamy of letting off Gould, a sudden jerk proclaimed that the engine was fastened to the train and after giving about half a dozen great screams and thereby quite exhausting itself it set off at a slow pace puffing puff puff-puff – In two minutes we were at full speed and in about twelve had reached our destination. By appointment we were to meet at the Old Hat. but Papa having found out that he had directed us wrong, came to the station, just as we were going off the wrong way. Mr Mayne took off his hat and cried out "Welcome to our country seat". We set out on our walk in the direction of Harrow. turned to the left and soon came to the gates of an old house that had been pulled down. It had a few traces of antiquity about it but we could not gain any information from a boy who was passing except that it was pulled down some years ago and that there was going to be a new one built up. The next place we came to was Perrivale. which is interesting on account of a church which is said to be very ancient in parts. We did not go close to it. but from the view on the road, it looked

46

very pretty. We then went to the viaduct at Hanwell which appeared to me a very fine thing, which is not at all extraordinary, it being pretty generally considered as such, and from thence along a road across two or three fields, to the Old Hat: where we made ourselves exceedingly comfortable with bread and

butter and ale which it is scarcely necessary to say tasted a great deal better than ordinary bread and butter or ale either, which is not at all to be wondered at when we consider the circumstance of their having been devoured in "an Old Hat and no mistake". At all events they disappeared with a velocity perfectly disgusting and we bid good bye to the Old Hat and set off home. We waited nearly half an hour at the station during which I had nothing to babbit to read that Stark the landlord of the "Feathers" had an Ordinary every Sunday at two, which was written up in large letters on the house and might be read for nothing any day. The train at last came up. We got in safely, came out without being damaged, went down a stone stair without breaking our bones and walked out on the road without being run over and then home without being tired, and so ended this memorable day.

47

Sunday. I was very glad to day when when I heard that we were to have a weeks holidays. because then perhaps I may get Quentin Durward finished.

Sunday This is Easter Sunday and Lent is over. After the show. Henry wanted to take a little puppy into the park so I accompanied him. It was a very fine day, great crowds out, and Mr Mayne came in the evening. It is a pity we did not get up a grand show to day.

Monday. At twelve oclock we all went to the Polytechnic Institution Now the Polytechnic Institution is a very pleasant place to spend four hours and a half in, and I should like to see the two legged animal who would say to the contrary. just so that I might examine his or her features. The chief object of interest was a diving bell in which Henry and I went down some twenty feet below the water, all the while suffering the most unpleasant sensations in the ears that can be con-ceived. while a little girl who was in the machine with us actually cried out right and the man who was with her made wry faces What a deli-

cious thing it would have been to have seen the wa-ter beautifully pouring in at a sweet little hole in the top. The next thing to be seen was a little fat man quite scarlet with the heat and exertion lecturing on the steam engine to a crowd of listeners, I wont say hearers for as I said before the little scarlet man was so excited either from the heat or somthing else that we could hardly hear a word he said. I witnessed the spectacle from a gallery and it had a very pleasing effect. Later in the day Mr Green gave a lecture on the babboon, that is the balloon. It was quite a mistake I put two b's in stead of l's. When a man roared out that this was to take place there was a general rush to get into the lecture room and I rushed amongst the rest. I had not gone far when in going up a stairs I was nearly pitched backwards on my head by the crowd before and the next moment almost on my nose by the rush behind. At last after the most desperate exertion I succeeded in reaching the door of the room and then to my infinite satisfaction found it crammed. After making two or three desperate leaps into the air on the progress of which I only caught a glimpse of the lecturers head I abandoned the attempt in despair, and went down stairs standing on all the peoples toes that were coming up. There are a great variety of miniature steam engines, electric shocks and et ceteras to be seen.

Tuesday. I have been most of the day making little figures for a Pantomime which Frank is going to act to night. After toiling at them all day I ran out for a short time and when I came home I found a

a little thing named Glandville in the house who was come to witness the performance of Bombastes Furioso and a new comic pantomine in two acts. All the characters to be supported by. Master Frank Doyle

The first peice went off rather tamely, but the pantomine called forth such peals of merriment from the wit displayed therein which was all brewed on the spot by the spirited manager, that I dont know what might not have happened if a supper had not been announced

WEDNESDAY 22d. James I and Henry went with F. Moore to Chanteys. I cant attempt a description of the numbers of fine statues busts and monuments which I saw there. but I liked best of all a monument in which was a widow and her daughter weeping over the grave of her husband. I think it was the most beautiful monument I ever saw Among the busts those of John Hunter Curran and Bird the artist. I liked best

Friday. 23d. Went out before breakfast. Mr Meyricks dog Laddie has come to town more working on Quentin, and at five took Tasso to Mr Rothwell who is going to bring it to Mrs Franklin Lewis. I then took a copy of the what you may call em to a gentleman in Russell square and saw the new number of Master Humpheys Clock. **Saturday.** I think I will do the death of sir Philip Sydney for my next history only then I dont like to begin it till I have finished. Quentin Durward which at first I expected to have had done at Easter but now find I may be another fortnight at it Shocking" I

can hardly stand. here we are to go to Harbours in less than a week When can I do it. **Sunday.** Went to eight oclock mass. sorry to say. not much of a show. As for me I am fastened to that great big thing Quentin Durward which might be a very fine thing in its way but at the same time keeps me from doing anything else, not that I want to begin.

one thing before I finish another, no that would be directly opposite to my principles (humbug) but that I happen at the present moment moment to be particularly anxious to go on with our new series of histories. which James and I are going to do and which anxiety is not materielly lessened by Papa's having promised to get them bound when finished to the number of thirty. We all went into Kensington Gardens and stayed there till three Nothing remarkable occurred with the exception of some extraordinary gestures of surprise on the part of some of the party, at the rapid appearance of leaves on the trees.

Went out before breakfast, home at half past eight I mean to make a rule of doing it every morning and by degrees get to be up at five and out at six. Grisi made her first appearance this season on Saturday night, in triumph according to the "Observer" Of course it was in triumph how could it be otherwise. I hear some people abusing her in such a terrible way that it is really a wonder how she could.

MAY.

RIDAY. 1st Here is a state of things no van dyke brown. I must give up up painting for want of a brown. I went to see the Queen going to the Exhibition. I am so tired of seeing them that I would not have gone only that I had a sort of melancholy pleasure in going to linger about the door of the Academy, pondering about what could be subject of McClise's large picture. besides there is always something pleasant in seeing the crowd and hearing the yell. The bells of St. Martins had been ringing for an hour when five state carriages drove up emptied themselves on the pavement at the door of the National Gallery where they were received by Sir Martin Archer Shee and forthwith carried up stairs and certainly I never envied the Queen so much as I did at that moment and for the next hour and a half. At all events Monday wont be long coming and then for the most glorious day of the year. Saturday. There was a most extraordinary riot at the Italian Opera house

House on Thursday evening. Several times during the opera there had been cries for Tamburini but as soon as it was over the uproar was tremendous

There were a party of nobleman in the omnibus box who with Prince G. of Cambridge (so says the paper) were the ringleaders. The orchestra attempted to play the overture to the ballet but was quite smothered in the deafening cries for Tamburini and Laporte. They tried several times but every time the first note was struck such a yell rent the air as might have startled a fat man even if he had been warned beforehand. Mr Laporte at length made his appearance amid a most desperate volley of screams while the majority of the house cried him down. every time he tried to speak others called out " No Tamburini" no intimidation." The manager in the mean time was carrying on a conversation with the occupants of the omnibus box but did not seem to come to a satisfactory conclusion, he retired, the drop curtain rose, and the dancers appeared but just as the orchastra struck the first note. one of the most terrible

outcries that were ever given vent to rang though the house. The manager was again forced to appear and attempted to make a speach but his voice was 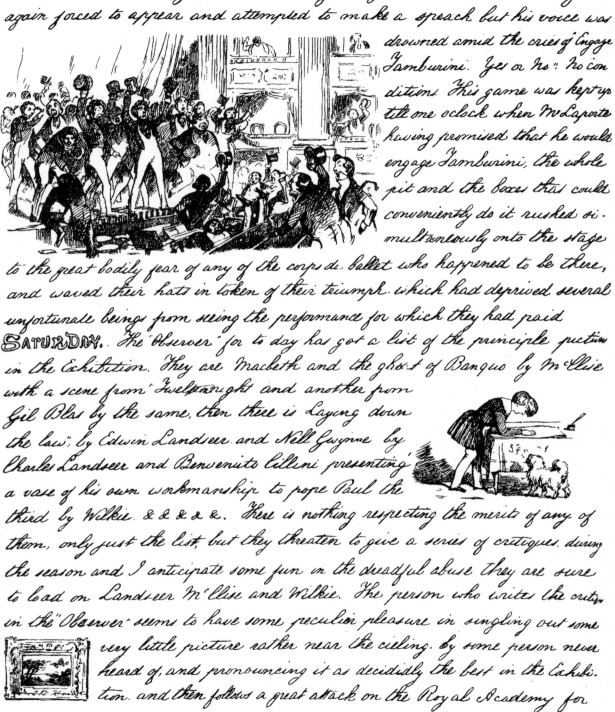 drowned amid the cries of Engage Tamburini. Yes or No. No conditions. This game was kept up till one oclock when Mr Laporte having promised that he would engage Tamburini, the whole pit and the boxes that could conveniently do it rushed simultaneously onto the stage to the great bodily fear of any of the corps de ballet who happened to be there, and waved their hats in token of their triumph. which had deprived several unfortunate beings from seeing the performance for which they had paid

SATURDAY. The "Observer" for to day has got a list of the principle pictures in the Exhibition. They are Macbeth and the ghost of Banquo by Mc Clise with a scene from "Twelfth night and another from Gil Blas by the same, then there is Laying down the law". by Edwin Landseer. and Nell Gwynne by Charles Landseer and Benvenuto Cellini presenting a vase of his own workmanship to pope Paul the third by Wilkie. & & & & &. There is nothing respecting the merits of any of them, only just the list, but they threaten to give a series of critiques. during the season and I anticipate some fun in the dreadful abuse they are sure to load on Landseer Mc Clise and Wilkie. The person who writes the critiques in the "Observer" seems to have some peculiar pleasure in singling out some very little picture rather near the cieling. by some person never heard of, and pronouncing it as decididly the best in the Exhibition. and then follows a great attack on the Royal Academy for

54

not putting it in the principle place. I wish tomorrow morning would come.

Monday 11. It
has come. at last. and at
half past ten (which was
a great deal too soon) James
Henry and I set out for
Trafalgar Square and
arrived of course half
an hour before the door
was opened. There was a
pretty considerable number of persons collected and they were increasing in most
rapid manner so we stood in the door way watching the clock and the different characters who came crowding up. Exactly at twelve the door burst open
and in we rushed, there was a great scramble to pay first and then off we
darted up the stairs. There were about fifty besides us in the first rush almost in a body. and we had a desperate race. I dont know who won it

but Henry was third
and I was fourth.
I rushed straight
down the rooms till
I came to Mc Elises
picture of Macbeth
and there I stopped.
At the first look it
appeared the best of
Mc Elises large pictures
for coloring but. pre-

55

sently I found out that the background was painted with some horrid color like ink. Macbeth himself is very fine and perhaps Lady Macbeth is also, but I am not sure. The drapery of both are beautiful and the torch bearers leaning forward to try and see what is frightening their master are capitally conceived. I wanted to see the principle pictures before the crowd got to great to move so I turned away from this and looked all round the room. There was a beautiful Landseer of a dog and parrot in the corner to the right which first caught my eye from the splendid coloring of the birds feathers, then a little farther that way Leslies portrait of Lord Cottenham then I looked over to the other side and easily discovered "Henry the 1st hearing of the shipwreck of his son" to be by Hart. from the purple and light yellow all over. which I dont like at all. Just below it was Nell Gwynne by Charles Landseer. Nell Gwynne is a beautiful figure but looks too nice a person. and the "Merry Monarch" the earl of Rochester and other lords look exactly like each other. I dont think the painting is as rich as

as Charles Landseer generally. The most extraordinary picture altogether is The Slave trade by a French artist quite unknown. For expression and drawing it is wonderful, the painting is not quite so pleasant though there is something appropriate and fine in the red sunset which covers nearly the whole sky. What a curious thing it is to think that there should be such a good artist quite unknown in England. Malvolio in the garden of Olivia by McClise is beautiful for expression but the general tone of the picture is of that cold green which Leslie has been so fond of lately, while the Gil Blas by

McClise also is decidedly one of his very best for color. How fine is Edwin Landseers Laying down the Law: as I turned from the last picture I could see the great great white dog over the peoples heads at the other side of the room and I dont think I ever saw anything more like nature or perhaps as much. There are at least twenty dogs heads in the picture and they are all life. What an extraordinary thing it is that some men can be found who deny the power of Landseer and compare such animals as Hancock to him. It seems incredible. I think it must be that Landseer being so generally admired they want to be original and therefore are always trying to find out some shabby little dogs or other quadrupeds that they say are superior to anything Landseer could do. There is a rather peculiar picture by W Etty of ten virgens running about in front of a door which is beautifully painted. The subject is taken from Scripture but the treatment is decidedly queer. The sculpture for this year is I think less interesting than any exhibition I remember.

Tuesday. By some fate or other it happens that I have not written any journal since last Monday which is rather a miserable business. I dont know how it is but once I get into that state, and I do very often I grieve to say, I dont really think I have the power to go on

Graf promised to send another fifty copies to day but did not I spent all the morning in painting Quenten Durward I hope to get it finished in a week At four I went to the band in Kensington Garden which began to play on Tuesday. The crowd was not very great at least to me, anyone who has not seen it in July might think it tremendous. The selection was not particularly good either but perhaps that arose from their only having the brass instruments, and consequently being obliged to play only marches and such things as can be conveniently played on horse-back However I hope they likely resume the other instruments next time otherwise it will be a most uncomfortable concern. besides it seems to be only just for the trouble bringing the music stand which is done by means of a cart At about six oclock an alarm was given that the Queen was coming along the road, the people simultaneously made a desperate rush at the wall and the band stopping short in the middle of what they were

playing and wheeling round struck up "God save the Queen" Her Majesty and Prince Albert were in the pony phæton. They passed the band twice.

Saturday Mr Street at 11 Two hours work on the Quentin Durward and then out. Glorious fun Mr Mayne wants five more copies

Sunday. Went to Mass at half past seven. The show chiefly consisted of Elgin marbles which we have been copying a great deal during the week James had a good part of a History and Henry had something in the painting way. the production of Frank and Charles were various. In the evening Mr Moore came and ordered a "Tournament" for one of Lord Denmans daughters.

MONDAY Frank Adelaide and Charles went to the Exhibition to day. and I spent the whole day in drawing and practising the Violin scales by turns. At about five the party came home. and their was nothing for more than an hour but a shower of opinions about the different pictures. but as I cant remember them all perhaps if I could they might fill the whole book, perhaps it would be better not to try to remember any.

Tuesday. I think I did more to Quentin to day than any day I can remember, that is since the very beginning for I did an enormous. quantity the first day I began to color it but it always seems more at the beginning of a picture than when it is more advanced. At all events I had the faces to do to day and any one must allow that they are the most difficult part of all. What a curious thing it is it has been raining all day. I declare it seems as if there had been a mistake in months and that May had come instead of April last month for it was the most beautiful weather throughout while there has scarcely been a day since the beginning of May. that it has not rained and been rather cold to boot.

Wednesday. At last they came. At eleven o'clock this day a stout man from Graf came armed with fifty copies of the Tournament but oh what a go the covers were all pasted up the back and were otherwise dirty. James went direct to speak about it and they promised another fifty to morrow. It is rather provoking after waiting so long for them.

THURSDAY. Quentin not done yet what a dreadful thing. Henry and I went into the park. when just as we got to the serpentine we heard the Life Guards band on the other side and that reminded me that there was

to be a Drawing Room
to day so off we scampered
and arrived in the park
in time to see the Queen
going to St James's palace
When I came home I took
three copies to M Mayne
and saw Prince Albert

in George S on his way to the Regents Park. His legs looked rather long.

60

FRIDAY. Work Work work rain rain rain Did you ever experience anything like it and in May to, to make the matter worse. I have been pain-
ing and practising the scale all day. I did an Elgin Marble after dinner
and in the evening (for I could not before from the rain) went out and
brought home the seventh number of Master Humphreys Clock.

SATURDAY. Went into the park directly after breakfast. The Scots Fusileers were

well ex

ercising

and

fired

for the

first

time

this

year. Mr Skeet came at 12. Mr Graf sent a man here this morning
and was paid for the fifty wrappers Papa and Uncle have gone to Ealing and wont be home till dinner to morrow. I went this evening
to Roney and Fosters but the shop was shut and I came home colorless

SUNDAY. Went to 7 oclock, home at 9. What a horrid day. pouring rain
and no chance of its clearing up and Papa and Uncle went to Ealing with
the intention of taking a long walk to day. What will they do. What will
I do. I cant go out. I dont like to draw and I dont want to do anything else that I know of. Papa and Uncle came home at five beautifully
soaked, after having walked the whole way home in what is called cats
and dogs. No one appeared in the evening.

MONDAY. Went to the Park before breakfast. Two battalions exercising
as usual. I spent the remainder of the day in working on the Quentin.

I went into the park for about half an hour. the cold was dreadful. I worked at my History till dinner and then took a Tournament to Mr Mayne. James went to hear an examination at the St Pauls School but could not get in because he was five minuttes late. However in the evening he went to the the Opera It is Don Giovani - the very one that James wanted to see of all others. **Friday.** Up rather early. When on earth is the fine weather going to come. An amusing incident took place in the pit of the Opera House last night. A great fat man wanted a gentleman to move farther up, the gentleman said he was with a which was in the bench before. the fat man said "That is nothing to the purpose will you move up or will you not, the gentleman said that the fat man might pass him if he wished. but this would not satisfy the fat man who again said "Will you move up or will you not." the gentleman said "Certainly not." The fat man would not pass the gentleman. which probably arose from a fear of being jamed in between the opposite bench and the gentleman if he attempted it, but he comforted himself with giving vent to his feelings in the following words "Whitechapel" evidently from Whitechapel" Case of excessive Whitechapel" and then got into very low spirits in which he continued the whole night only varying the monotony of it by every now and then darting a feirce look

62

or grunt over his shoulder, at the gentleman who preserved a digni-
fied silence and could not be prevailed upon even to look at the great
fat man in spite of all his grunts and fierce looks.

SATURDAY. Henry and I have made a rule to go out for one hour
regularly every morning. Mr Mayne came in the evening and cut up
Don Giovanni in a most shocking manner that is he cut up Grisi Tam
brini and Persiani and I am not sure that Rubini was not among
them. Now I recollect I am sure he was.

 Nine oclock mass. Rained almost all day. Mr Moore came to
dinner and we had the show in the evening. Henry had a copy of the crew of
the Medusa on the raft. I had half a history but wont show it till next week
when I expect to have it finished. Frank Adelaide and Charles contributed largely

MONDAY. 25th The Queens birthday. I went to the park at nine and not seeing any exercising going on I began to suspect that there might be an inspection in front of the Horse Guards and just then hearing a band at the other side
of the park Henry I and Ruff started off and caught a regiment in full dress

entering St James's. I now began to think my suspicions correct particularly as we met another battalion making for the same point. We arrived on the parade in front of the Horse Guard and there all doubt was quickly dispelled for what should be seen coming along the park but a company of Life Guards with their band. It now became pretty plain that an inspection was about to take place and that of a very high order. Lord Hill soon appeared, and was quickly followed by the duke who came in a chaise and then mounted his little fat bay horse. There were a considerable number of officers now collected among

whom were the dukes of Cambridge and Marquess of Londonderry but still it was rather plain that some one else was expected. Just then my eye caught somthing brilliant shining through the trees and the next instant Prince Albert at the head of a glittering staff appeared galloping up the road. As soon as they came on the ground. the duke and lord Hill rode to meet him and after placing themselves on either side of him rode up the line all the bands playing "God save the Queen". The troops then went by in slow and quick time and a shower of rain coming on

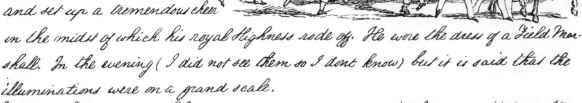

the business was speedily brought to a close. The moment it was over the people who by this time recognised the prince all rushed into the middle of the parade and set up a tremendous cheer in the midst of which his royal Highness rode off. He wore the dress of a Field Marshall. In the evening (I did not see them so I dont know) but it is said that the illuminations were on a grand scale.

Tuesday & Wednesday. These two unfortunate days are totally unprovided for How I came to omit them in the original M S is and ever must remain unknown to the world.

Thursday. I am working hard at Edward VIth granting charters which I want to finish by Sunday. I went to Ackermans and bought a sketch book for James Papa went to Ealing at five and Adelaide has got Miss Kate Glandville to tea.

Friday the 29th of May. Mr Skeel came to day instead of tomorrow. I went early this morning to get the Philomen Waltz for James and Annette and while I was in the shop I saw twelve of Strauss's waltzs arranged for the violin. so says I give it up' and it was immediately given and I paid sixpence (rather expensive) After dinner we all sallied out to the band in Kensington Gardens. The Queen Dowager and a great party of equestrians were inside on the grass. The place was very crowded. After tea I left a note at Mr Dickensons and then went for The Clock.

Saturday. A messenger from Dickensons came this morning for six copies.

All this week I have been doing a picture of the review on Monday. and of course am very glad when it turned out that Papa likes it. Heres fun by the twelve oclock past to day a note arrived directed to Master Dick Doyle. I hastily tore open the document and found it to contain an order from Mr Moore for six Tournaments. I brought them of course. Was ever anything equal to it since the beginning of the

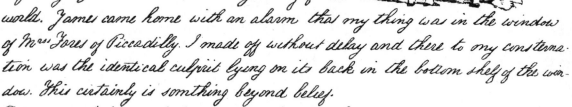

world. James came home with an alarm that my thing was in the window of Mrs Fores of Piccadilly. I made off without delay and there to my consternation was the identical culprit lying on its back in the bottom shelf of the window. This certainly is something beyond belief.

Sunday. 31st. Nine oclock Mass. At the show had part of Prince Albert reviewing the footguards in front of the Horse Guards and Edward VI granting charters.

JUNE

MONDAY. I have been expecting this day with some anxiety from an inkling I had that I might go to Eliasons concert which is to take place to night Owing to this I was kept in a pleasing flutter of uncertainty for a great portion of the day. I attempted to paint but in vain so I threw down the brush and did not know what to do. Even the Tower of London for June would not comfort me though I did contrive to get through it somehow or other I went out at nine to see the Treasury which I am going to introduce into the background of my picture of the review. In St James's Park I met Mr Mayne and was talking with him for some time. I came home at twelve and at three how great was my joy when all doubt was dispelled and it was declared that I was to go. but as I wont be home till one and will then most likely be too tired to write. I have written this before I go and must write an account of the concert tomorrow.

TUESDAY 2. The concert was glorious. Of the singers Dorus Gras stands first both in execution and every thing else She sang "Oh Tourment" from Aubers opera "Le Serment" beautifully. There is an ernest and impassioned manner about her which is particularly delightful more particularly when contrasted with the coldness of many of the English singers who come out and sing with their eyes fixed on the music the whole time, in a kind of quiet

67

misery, pretending they are only reading the song for the first time when most likely they know them quite off by practice. The room was not very far off from being crammed to suffocation and was plentifully besprinkled with Jews. The crack  piece of the evening was a duet between Eliason and Litz. It was a concerto of Beethovens and the last movement was one of the most beautiful things I ever heard. Litz also played a Grand Valse de Bravoura and being rapturously encored therin came out again and thundered away at the Tarantula which from the extraordinary number of notes contained in it I should suppose by far the most wonderful piece of difficulty. I ever saw or heard of Mr John Parry sung wanted a Governess and being encored did the Musical Wife. The German chorus which could not come till after the opera arrived at about half past eleven and sung three choruses two from Der Freischitz and one from Euryanthe. They were twice encored and had rather a good appearance with their blue jackets and collars turned down.

Tuesday. I mean Wednesday. Henry and I went into the park to have a sketch of some of the horses which with men on their backs or vehicles behind them swarm the roads particularly about Hyde Park corner. Unfortunately we returned without doing anything, for whenever I picked out an animal and had just opened the book, it would gallop away.

Thursday. I have been designing and beginning a history of the battle of Chalgrove. in which Prince Rupert made one of his desperate charges. so I have chosen the time when the Puritans under the influence of one of them are retreating. and the brave but rash prince is taking one of the banners. The Puritans afterwards won the battle

68

Friday. The occurences of this day are so much like what I have written so often that with the exception of the band in Kensington Gardens there is no need to say anything

Saturday. Nothing but work by day out by evening and violin by night.

Sunday. Nothing particular at the show. After it a long walk. No one in the evening.

Monday. Henry and I walked out this morning with the intention of going to the park but we had hardly got outside the door when there appeared an officer of the Blues riding slowly along the road. What a number of sensations are created by the sight of one officer of the Blues riding slowly along on a beautifully hot morning. The first idea that rushes on the mind is that a review is about to take place and you are thrown into a flutter of delight, then comes the reaction, you say "It cant be it is nothing." but in a few minutes you again become reassured and say "But then what would he be going along in his state dress for." besides where else could he be going." By this time you have reached the end of the road, and are thrown into an agony of hope, doubt, and apprehension. The person you are with strongly advises going. You stop and with a painful interest watch the progress of the officer as he slowly rides out of sight. suddenly you cry out "I will go. and in another minute are seen making in the direction of Jacksons grounds

at the rate of five miles an hour at least. We (for it is exactly our case)
burst into the field in less than ten minutes. and if ever there was a
beautiful morning this was it when we burst into those fields. Imagine
the most beautiful of suns shining in such a manner as to make every
thing look yellow, then the smell of the trees and grass which was so delightful, that the feeling of the country air which was calculated to make a person lie down on their back and kick, only that from the excessive heat
of the weather the exercise would be too violent. It was while walking
along the side of a hedge, in the full enjoyment of all the delightful sensations just discribed, that the distant sound of trumpets burst at once upon
our ears. It proceeded from the direction of Notting Hill. all doubt was
at once dispelled, and we could plainly see the glittering cuirasses of the
of the Life Guards sparkling in the sun. We hastened on to the ground
and their to our joy found a regiment of Lancers. who had dismounted.
I was walking along looking at the Life Guards who were coming up when
I was suddenly made aware of the presence of some extraordinary per-

70

sons. by a tremendous volley of oath which were let loose on some unknown person or thing. and turning round at the explosion. I found

myself in the immediate neighbourhood of a party of Lancer officers
They were distinguished gentlemen. because they frequently called each other
"My Lord" but if ever I heard curious conversation those gentlemen were
the perpetrators of it. At half past ten Col Cavendish having previously
given directions to all the principal officers, the line was formed and
shortly afterwards Prince Albert came on the ground with a large staff.
including Lord Hill the duke of Cambridge Prince George of Cambridge. Lord
Alfred Paget and quantities of others whom I did not know, and three
Austrian hussas to give a novelty to it The duke of Wellington came
afterwards. At a few minutes before eleven Prince Albert rode up
the line. the cavalry then went past him in slow and quick time
and then all galloped past in lines. The manœuvreing then began

and was kept up in a most spirited manner for an hour and a half. One of the evolutions was particularly pretty and was done to a nicety. The heavy cavalry were slowly advancing in three divisions, with as much space between each as the length of each division when suddenly the lancers who had also formed into three divisions then galloped up through the three spaces left by the Life Guards. This was no sooner done then the Lancers spread out and began to fire their carbines. The retreat was sounded they formed into the three divisions as before and galloped through the spaces left, with such precision, though at full speed that there was not room for a single other man. As the business concluded and the salute given, Prince Albert called all the officers about him and proceeded to compliment them on their different regiments. When it came to this we judged it prudent to to make haste to the gate and await the Prince's exit. As an example of the heat there was a boy selling dirty (it looked like ditch) water out of a pail at a halfpenny a mugfull. When we reached the gate we found the band of the Life Guards waiting to play his Royal Highness out. First came the regiment of Blues then the Lancers then a great number of carriages in which

72

were many of the officers, who had dismounted. The duke also came in a carriage but just as Prince Albert was nearing the gate he dismounted with about a dozen other officers and began to toil slowly up the steep bank

and on to the railway and forthwith to inspect the rails closely. There was no guard to keep the people off and the consequence was that in a few minutes they were surrounded a mob of about two hundred persons chiefly countrymen and workmen of the railway. He seemed very interested for he was quite a quarter of an hour and appeared to be talking to the workmen. At last he came down, mounted and rode amid one of the greatest cheers I ever heard

Tuesday. Of course as is always the case after such things. I had a great desire to do a picture of it, but as my one of the foot inspection is not finished I wont begin it yet. I worked at my History most of the day and after dinner went to the band. They play a very nice set of Musards Quadrilles called the Rendezvous de Chase.

WEDNES. At two oclock to day Mr Rothwell Papa James Henry and I all went to the Hippodrome. This was the first day they have had this year and from the list of horses on the cards promised to be the best they have

had in point of racing. Great numbers of people were present and some
stylish turns out among which Lord Pembrokes was
conspicuous. There were also The Marquess of Westmins
ter Lords Wilton, George Bentinck Orford Alfred Paget
&cc Gen Grosvenor Col Anson Col Peel and Mr Greville.
The first race was won by a horse named Bedford
beating the second by a neck and the third by a length
the others being well up. He won the second heat rather easier. As
the horses came out for the second Papa guessed which would win and
which would be second. The next race which was the principal one of the
day was not so interesting though the horses were superior. It was won by
Mr Keens Fitzroy beating Daedalus Dreadnaught and Nonsense &cc The stakes
were at least eight hundred pounds. The third race was not so good as
either of the others but still was well contested, the three first horses being nearly
abreast at the Stewards Stand. I forget the name of the winner. At about
three oclock the hill presented a most brillant appearance being covered with

74

FRIDAY I went this morning to have a look at the fatal wall where the shot is said to have entered I stared at the spot for a few minutes but not feeling a bit the wiser I came home

Saturday. There is an annual concert which takes place at the Opera House. I dont know what is the particular meaning of it but this was the night and Uncle sent me out to try and get a look at a pro-grame. I had a good deal of trouble to do it and at last found one about half way down Oxford Street. I came home and told Uncle the con-

tents and he in return told me I was to go with him. We set off with the intention of being in time but not of having to wait at the door for twenty minutes, which was the case. A rumbling of iron bars is suddenly heard and the doors burst open and in rush the people. Three minutes desperate corporal exertion took us into the pit. The concert began with Beethovens Pas--torale symphony which was better done then uncle ever heard before Grisi's "Bel raggio" from Semeramide and Persiani in a new song from Ines de Castro were both to my mind perfect, whatever they might have been in reality. Ru bini sung I should say gave a beautiful song of Mercadante's which was so beautiful that I could hardly hear a word of it from its extreme piano It ended with the celebrated duet from Matrimonio Segreto in which both

75

Tamburini and Lablache performed. This is the first time I have heard the Opera company for more than two years and was consequently a great treat

Friday. Dickenson sent for a dozen copies this morning. he has sold the half dozen he had. I had only six to give him and must order a new fifty to morrow.

Saturday. Hard work is the thing. I want to get this history done by sunday and am afraid I wont be able. It has been in progress a long time and it is quite time it was off the board. Ordered the fifty this evening

Sunday. Went out and got the 'Observer.' Nothing particular at the show M. A Selous came in the evening and sang two new songs of Shubert which he brought with him

Monday  Went to the park till ten. an inspection of one battalion of the Scots Fusiliers. Lord Hill. Come home and put the paper on the board for tomorrow. Went out again after dinner to make a sketch in the park. Great crowds. Queen drove round three times

Tuesday. 23ᵈ Tutor at eleven. Began the third number of the History of Belgium. I have been into town for uncle and am terribly tired

SUNDAY. Mr Mayne came to breakfast went out for a walk with with Papa came home. had the show. James had Richard the second knighting the fish kings and I had a portrait of Charles and Edward the sixth granting charter to the founder of the Bluecoat school. Just before Mr Mayne went he gave me a five pound note for all the copies of the Tournament he has disposed of which leaves me in full possesion of one pound two and six. Glorious

Monday. I have been getting my history of granting the charters in to such

a wretched state. thas it is doubtful whether it will ever survive it. The lord mayors face is the centre of the mischief

Wemesday. The Queen went to Ascot yesterday which was the first day of the races. Prince Albert and the Prince of Leiningen were with her in the first carriage, in the second was M Guizot the Duchess of Beaufort & &c and at least ten other royal carriages followed The Gold vase was won by Mr Petits St Francis (Robinson). beating Mulatto and lord Exeters Amarath. I went to Finch lane to get James some numbers of the life of Napoleon but the man said could not get them till tomorrow morning so as I did want to have to go all that way again I went to Paternoster row and after a little trouble got them for it is difficult to get the number anywhere except at the publishers. The bill of fare for the gold cup looks well provided all the horses run. It includes Bloomsbury S᷑ Francis Caravan Euclid Valentissimo and Flambeau.

Wednesday I mean Thursday. The guards were in the park this morning in state dress although there was no inspection. Another fifty of the Tournament came home this morning "Come" something like, makes a hundred and fifty in all At the same time another three pound ten goes out of my pocket. If I could go to Norma for half a crown I really would give it at this moment.

Friday. The great day came and went yesterday in the presence of the Queen and Prince Albert. Papa went down by the Great Western at eight. Crowds immense. The cup was won by S᷑ Francis beating Caravan who won it last year beating S᷑ Francis Bloomsbery who won the Derby was second. his not being first is to be attributed to the great weight he was obliged to carry. Euclid was last. Thimble rigs abounded. Gambling booths without number. Company in the promenade not so select as formerly, quite as plentiful. M Guizot the French ambassador made himself very

conspicuous in the Queens stand Went to Kensington Gardens in the hope of a band. Was none. Went and got Master Humphreys Clock Came home and found that James and Annette had gone to Ma᷑ Verini's concert and a ticket for me. Just eight now. its beginning. Rushed off.

78

JULY.

WEDNESDAY. I don't understand the meaning of this. Here the officers of the blues have taken it into their heads to prevent the band playing in the Gardens on Tuesdays and Wednesdays. There was a general change of Barracks about a fortnight ago, the Life Guards who were here going to Windsor, those that were at Windsor coming to the Regents Park and the Blues who were there going to the Knightsbridge barracks and when they get there refusing to do what both the regiments of Life Guards have always done and what they themselves always did other years when it came to their turn. I dont see what is the sense of it. Are the officers jealous of their band being heard so often. If so I cant help thinking that it is very foolish. If not, what in the name of wonder is the reason. Alas and is this the way we are to be cheated out of nearly two months of Tuesday and Friday afternoonly bands. This morning when I was over near the barracks I saw two of the officers talking smoking and leaning against the railings,

79

I declare it was with the greatest difficulty I could prevent myself from rushing upon them, and asking what they meant by the manner in which they had

been behaving themselves. If the matter requires to be made worse, this will do it. The very instrumentalists ride up and down, in front of the barracks, almost every morning for about about half an hour, at ten oclock, either for the purpose of entertaining the officers at their breakfast, or just for practice, instead of doing it in doors, perhaps it is for both purposes. Now I should not be surprised if some person possessing a superabundance of wisdom and shrewdness was to say "Would not it be just as well to hear them play in the morning as in the afternoon "particularly as it takes place almost every day, which would made up for its being only for half an hour " Let all such persons know that while on foot they perform the most beautiful of Bellini's airs, Musards Quadrills and Strauss's Waltzs, and while on horseback only march's and such like. I will now bid fare well to this disgusting subject. I am very hard at work this week on a "history" of the Norwegian soldier who when fighting against Harold defended a narrow wooden bridge for four hours, when he was killed by a javelin

THURSDAY.

2ᵈ This morning at ten oclock James Henry I and Francis Moore set off for the Tower of London. We arrived at the lodge wherein tickets are procured at a few minutes before twelve. went from hence across a yard through a dark gateway over a drawbridge through another gate up one hill down another, turn to the left, one more gate known by the name of the gateway to the "bloody Tower" and then we are at the entrance to the horse armorey. The ticket being shown to a stout warder we were handed into the custody of another warder equally stout though. whose instrumentality we were forthwith conveyed into the edifice. The unsophisticated visitor is instantaneously impressed with awe at finding himself in the immediate presence of nearly a hundred armed horsemen who appear only waiting for the word of command. to spring upon the assembled spectators and totally annihilate them

81

but in a short time the feeling wears off and gives way to great admiration. The Horse Armoury (commonly called) is an apartment of about three hundred

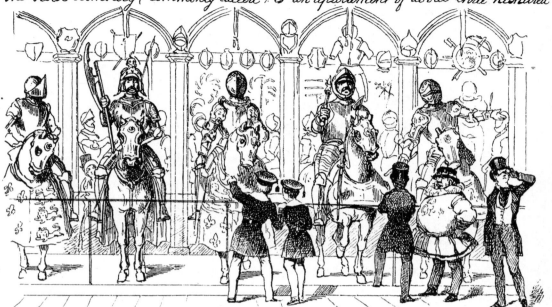

feet in length, containing as I said before about a hundred armed horsemen. together with numberless suits of steel armours and helmets, curasses and weapons of all descriptions, not to mention the ceiling and walls being covered with fire arms so arranged as to form ornaments such as stars &c. Here we have the complete suit of ring armour of the reign of Stephen and the splendid fluted armour of the time of Henry the VIII, the mail jacket said to have been worn by Saladin and the cuirass shattered by cannon ball from the feild of Waterloo. About half way up the room stands a body of about forty men in complete suits of iron armoursaid to be the body guard in the time of Charles the first The horsemen represent the kings of England from the time of Edward the 1st up to James the IIᵈ. There are also many distinguished noblemen such as Charles Brandon duke of Suffold &c. The most gorgeous suit of armour in the collection is that worn by Henry the eight, which is covered with embossed gold.

We next entered a room called Queen Elizabeth's armoury so named from the fact of that distinguished sovereign being seated on horseback at the farthest extremity similing blandly on all around and led by a small page the while. The walls are almost wholly covered with sheilds swords harquebuss's spears lances and partizans The variety and design of the spear heads is quite remarkable, some of them are beautiful. I can not believe that this is the same room as used to be called the Queen Elizabeth. In the Penny Magazine there is a view of it, which represents an apartment at least four times as large as the one of which I speak, besides having a row of thin pillars at each side, which it has not. I suppose an alteration has taken place in the arrangement. Among other interesting objects in this collection is to be seen the block on which the unfortunate earl of Derwentwater and his accomplicess were beheaded together with the foul implement which the deed was done. It is amusing to hear the stout Warder describing these and such like destructive instruments, in his pompous way

83

just as if he had lived in those times and remembered all the circumstances perfectly, while a crowd of anxious listeners stand looking on with faces of the greatest consternation. In this same room there is an opening in the wall which discovers a portion of the anciant stone wall, whereon is written divers names of unfortunate prisoners condemned to death which must have been done when the apartment was used as a state prison. If I recollect rightly Sir Walter Raleigh's was among them. Some of the names were accompanied by two or three appropriate lines. Close beside this interesting phenomenon, a very narrow door, scarcely more than a foot wide and looking so exactly like the rest of the wall that you could not by any possibility have guessed there was a door there, leads into one of the cells in which I suppose the prisoners slept. It was about six feet square, very low and the walls covered with writing all of which facts impressed the spectators with such awe that it was with the greatest difficulty any of the ladies could be persuaded to enter. To be sure once you entered, which was done by means of descending two steps, and being almost in total darkness, accompanied by a very damp smell you began to consider the possibility of the narrow doors banging to if I may use the expression

and even if it did not do it of its own accord which perhaps it would not, being so small and probably timid with strangers, there appeared to be every reason to suspect (and it would be only in keeping with his previous strange conduct) that the stout Warder, who must know all the secrets of the place, and probably had the keys secreted on his person, would make a sudden rush upon the door, shut it with a crash lock it, double lock it, put the keys in his pokets and walk away with an exulting laugh, in spite of the screams and yells of the wretched victims he had left to perish. then indeed it becomes alarming Shortly after this we left this part of the Tower altogether and crossing over the Green we entered a more modern looking pile, the interior of which presented to the eye an immense assemblage of ship heads, Union Jacks, cannons and marine stores of all descriptions, from hence we went up a stairs. very much decorated with the Union Jacks before mentioned and arrived in a spacious hall where we were first arrested by the sight of Lord Nelsons coat under a glass case, secondly by two very beautiful cannons of Indian manafature taken from Tipoo Saib, I believe, and thirdly by the uncommon appearance of at least twenty thousand muskets. fifty thousand I should say with more truth. The examining of these warlike instruments did not take long there being a certain degree of monotony about them and we came down stairs again. to examine some of the very extraordinary great cannons which were there Most of them were Indian, taken at

85

Seringapatam, many of them were Portuguese and a few were French. Having nothing more to see we walked deliberately out of the gate and said good bye to the Tower When we were crossing the Green we found the band of the grenadier guards playing in a ring for the edification of some of the officers and their ladies. This was very pleasant so we stopped for about a quarter of an hour to listen and then set off at a good round pace stopped at the first biscuit shop we came to, supplied ourselves, and then walked out to take a view of the Thames found that it was quite safe, recrossed the drawbridge, got some ginger beer (very refreshing) and then set off for the West end in right earnest. We found it too much by the time we reached the bank, so we got into a new road omnibus and were dragged along as far as Tottenham Court road. got out. went to Mr Moores to dinner, came home at about nine. found Mr Mayne here and playing the Russian hymn for the first time as we came into the room. Not being what would be termed over fresh after so much exercise, I soon went to bed.

FRIDAY. 8ᵗʰ When I awoke this morning I was assailed by a most uproarious discharge of musketry. My ears attempted to convince me it was going on in the street below, but my reason said it was really in the Park. To sleep under these trying circumstances (if I had wanted which I did not) would have been impossible so I rolled out of bed dressed, breakfasted hastily, and together with Henry and Ruff rushed in the direction of Hyde Park. Arrived there, I discovered a battalion of the Scots Fusiliers behaving very active-ly in that particular branch of service, known as "sharp shooting". The sharp shooters be it known are those persons who, in the exciting diversion called war, instead of keep-ing in lines or squares, fly about the ground in parties of two and three, first skip-ping behind a tree, popping out again, falling down dead, dancing up a hill and then dancing down again. Their "sharpness" is to consist in picking out some distinguished officer in the enemies ranks, presenting a musket at him, in such a way, that when discharged the contents be brought to bear upon his body thereby causing

87

immediate annihilation if possible. In the present instance being armed only with cartridges they did not commit any such atrocities Now it so happened that Ruff being provoked by the continued roar of musketry that was kept up, barked herself hoarse as a means of preventing it and being parched therewith we took her down into the gravel pit that she might drink of the waters it containeth. Scarcely had had gone down "down when a noise like nothing else in the world just over our heads impressed us with the fearful belief that the military were upon us. This was too true, before a minute had elapsed at least a company came clambering down and running over the gravel hills firing as they went while Ruff taking the alarm, to our immense consternation ran barking at them like mad. The retreat however was soon sounded, and put an end to the fray. the dog keeping up barking with all her mights and even rushing at their heels, till the last soldier disappeared from the pit. After this excitement she plunged into the Serpentine and swam almost a quarter way across.

SATURDAY. There was a grand inspection of the footguards in the Park this

88

morning at ten oclock. You may be sure we did not bring Ruff. The duke of Wellington came on the ground at a few minutes past ten. was met by Lord Hill. the

duke of Cambridge and a large staff and proceeded up the line after which the guards passed bye in slow and quick time. The firing then commenced and was kept up with great spirit for an hour and a half. the salute was then given and the duke proceeded home amidst great cheering. The crowd followed him. the whole way up to his door. the cheers which were intermingled with cries of "Waterloo" never ceasing. The band have got a very pleasant habit of playing in a ring after inspections which I totally approve of. They performed "Robert toi qui j'aime" to day beautifully. and afterwards the overture to Fra Diavolo.

SUNDAY 10. At the "show" this morning I had my "history" of Alfred in the Danish camp James had a number of Tasso and Henry a sketch from nature Annette had one flower and Frank and Charles had so many works of art that I could not mention them. We stayed in Kensington Gardens till three oclock. Mr Moore came in the evening.

Monday. 11th Here is a glorious piece of work. Fores a man residing in Piccadilly corner of Sackville street, keeping a printshop and being a publisher has sent me an order to do half a dozen envelopes. on Transfer paper. He has sent some designs which he wishes to have done, namely. Courting Coaching Hunting and Racing but I have got myself to design a Dancing and a Musical envelope James is going to do three and I three.

Tuesday 12. As soon as I came home from the park, I prepared all the

Transfer materials and set to work with great vigour. By evening I had finished the "Coaching" one, and James the "Hunting" and they will be sent to the printer's to-

morrow but now comes the designing part of the business. Wednesday. Nothing but work work work work all day I have made a design for the "Musical" one which Papa says will do, and James has almost finished another I went out after dinner and saw the duke and duchess of Nemours in the park the former riding with Prince Albert and the latter in the carriage with the Queen. Thursday. It is quite extraordinary the number of inspections that take place in the mornings now. It is very cheerful to see the old Duke in the park at ten oclock on his little cob, galloping about. Lord Hill was waiting for nearly a quarter of an hour this morning expecting him Two or three Aid de Camps were sent from him down to Apsly House and from Apsly house to him, at last an object is seen approaching from afar which as it draws near dis-closes the features of the hero of Waterloo, mounted upon an animal of small pro-portions which contrives to jog him into the air in an awful manner while he calmly surveys the sky above his head and appears as if he did not know where he was going. As he rode up he cried out "How dye do Hill I hope I have not kept you waiting" and being answered in the negative, they turned about and rode up the line which must have been ready to drop by that time having been standing waiting in a broiling sun for full half an hour. When it was all over and just as we were following the duke home that we might add a few cheers, I was surprised by a slap on the shoulder and turning round beheld to my joy and astonishment, a human youth by name Henry Jones who lived on our Terrace some

five or six years ago and whom I always entertained a particular regard for He had only just come to London lived in Dorset street Regents Park and was going shortly to a school in France. As he had never been in the national gallery, we proposed to go there, and he consented so we went. Bye the bye one of the new pictures, a Franciscan Friar by Rembrant is I think as fine a head as ever I saw, the design is so simple and the affect so beautiful. I think it is equal to the Rembrant Jew aye or the Gavartius either though I dont think many will

91

agree with me there. After examining the new Raffaelle very minutely for about a dozen times I really cannot find out anything very wonderful in it that is that at least twenty other men could not do as well as if not better. I am frightened at

having said this and yet I can not help thinking it. Rubenss picture of the brazen serpent of the wilderness is in some respects as fine as any of works I... in the national Gallery but it is nearly spoiled by the extreme grossness of the female figures It appears as if he had studied to make them as ugly as he could The figure of Moses is very grand and the man in the faeground lying with the snake about him is one of the finest things I ever saw.

Friday. The proofs of the four envelopes have come home, three of them will do but the fourth." The Musical" in consequence of the number of figures. the lines have got confused and some, not printed at all so I will have to do it over again. When James does the" Courting "one and I do this and the" Dancing "which is nearly finished as it is. they will be all done, and then comes the profits' hurra".

Saturday. I was working very hard before breakfast. and quite finished the dancing one by twelve and if I can only get the other done this evening it will

be a glorious thing. all done in one week. There is a picture by Hilton illustrating the "Fairie Queene" which is going to be bought by subscription and placed in the National Gallery. six hundred pounds is the price demanded. It is on view now in the private apartments in the Royal Academy and may be seen on application. Sunday. What took place to day is exactly like most other Sundays, that there no use recording it. Mr Selous came in the evening and sung a new song.

MONDAY. Francis Moore asked us to go with him to Mr Shaws, a gentleman who is just going to bring out a work called dresses and decorations of the middle ages. We went and were very much entertained for about an hour looking over his drawings, some of which are very curious, particularly the ancient rooms. The work will

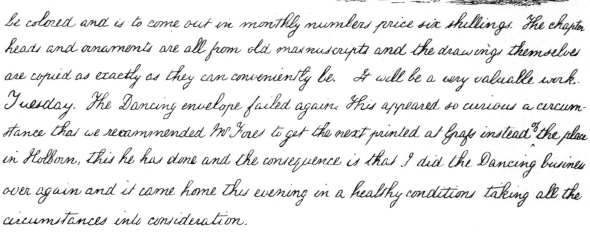

be colored and is to come out in monthly numbers price six shillings. The chapter heads and ornaments are all from old manuscripts and the drawings themselves are copied as exactly as they can conveniently be. It will be a very valuable work. Tuesday. The Dancing envelope failed again. This appeared so curious a circumstance that we recommended Mr Fores to get the next printed at Grafs instead the place in Holborn, this he has done and the consequence is that I did the Dancing business over again and it came home this evening in a healthy condition, taking all the circumstances into consideration.

Wednesday. "Hurra" I have got a light blue purse lined with white, and ornamented with ivory rings, and tassels attached to each end. actually groaning under the weight of coin, fit to bust itself. Most assuredly it would be only a charity to hasten unto the romantic region of Finch Lane, Cornhill. there to ease it of its load, by disposing of its contents in numbers of the History of France, illustrated

Thursday. We went with Francis Moore to see Hiltons picture to day. The subject is from Spencers Fairy Queen. where Serina is lying on the faggots just going to be

sacrificed by a party of wretches, and is rescued by Sir Calaphine who rushes upon them and kills every one. The figure of Serina is beautiful, the priests very spirited, the coloring rich and the figure of the knight himself. the only thing in it I dont like, There is somthing unpleasant in the look of the right arm. I dont know how it will look in the midst of the Titians of the National Gallery. but as it appears now, I own I think the landscape is worthy of Rubens himself.

Friday. 22° Mr Mayne went to Germany yesterday. that is he set off, after having previously introduced to Papa one Col Shultze who is coming to breakfast tomorrow. I went to Finch lane this afternoon and procured a glorious quantity of my book.

AUGUST.

FRIDAY. Well now that is something. To think of the duke of Orleans sending over a horse to win nearly the first race in England. It is quite true The Goodwood cup has been won by the Duke of Orleans Beggarman ridden by Robinson. and the Duke and Duchess of Nemours being present to make the thing more comfortable I remember that same Beggarman in the Derby of the year 1838 when Amato won. He belonged to Lord Shadbroke. The race next in importance was won by Lord Eglintouns. Potentate. beating the Beggarman, though the latter in the race for the cup beat some of the first horses in England, Euclid Charles the XII. &... **Saturday.** Ruff swims very lettely in the mornings now. It is a very queer thing that though the band of the Blues wont play in the Gardens in the afternoons they ride up and down on the green in front of the barracks playing for an hour or two every morning. I have been copying one of Juliens litho-graphic heads as large as life this week and have also two small portraits of James and Frank. I cant help having dislikings of the History of France somtimes. This afternoon was one of those times, so what do I do to cure it but go off and buy four more numbers, which cirtainly was a very effec-tual way of doing the business. The illustrations are some of the best I have got. At present I do one pages in the book with the marble over every evening. **Sunday.** Papa and Col Shultze went to Windsor this morning at nine and the show was consequently postponed till evening. We were hanging

over the balcony watching for their return till nearly nine. and had so sooner come in then they came. Col Shultze was delighted with Windsor Castle and thought it by far the finest thing of the kind he had seen. Frank and Charles figured most conspicuously in the show, and the rest of the evening was divided between conversation the piano, Col Shultze's voice, supper and the violincello.

Monday. 4th The heat is tremendous. The moment I rose (what a disgusting word) I did not rise I got up and the minute I did I knew it would be. There was the sky. one mass of dull blue, not a single cloud to be seen. and what is the consequence. why that I could hardly move. I reached home, after a crawl to the Serpentine with some difficulty and did not stir the remainder of the day except when I found it necessary to accompany my cries for water with a shower of kick

Tuesday. No inspection in the Park. very sad business. Began Cornelius Nepos with Mr Steet. finished my history of the seizure of the Duke of Northumberland and took it off the board. Col Shultze is up stairs in the Drawing Room singing one of his own songs while Annette is playing it at sight

96

and I who could not afford to spend my time in such trifles am down
here working away at an infernal journal. What a melancholy case
is Dick Doyles

WEDNESDAY. 6" Yesterday afternoon we went to Kensington Gardens to see if
their was a chance of the bands playing, but they did not I suppose that
the officers of the Blues are jealous of their band being heard

Thursday. Papa and Col Shultz went to Richmond this morning. No sooner had
Papa gone when a letter came for him which he having expected before he set
out it was deemed advisable to convey it to him if possible For this purpose
I set out at the top of my speed hoping to catch him at Zicours hotel in
S' Martins Lane where Col Shultz is staying and where Papa was to meet
him. I arrived at about ten minutes to eleven, rushed in and cried "Have two
gentlemen just gone." "Yes" I rushed out and down the Strand as far as
Hungerford Stairs and back again without once taking breath. I then began
to consider what I should do and decided on going first into the National
Gallery to see the new Murrillo (which is beautiful) and then home, both
of which I did, suffering intense mental agony the whole time from a
conviction that I must have passed them both in S' Martins lane. though
I had not the slightest ground for supposing I had done any thing of
the kind. At six in the evening I was going to Roney and Fosters for
some colors for Annette when I met Henry
who had just been seeing a placard thus
So therefore in the hope of a good days sport
(I mean evenings) I put off getting the
colors till tomorrow, and in company with
Henry set off for the ground. At first from
a number of people returning we thought
it must be all over but on enquiry we found
that the racing was, but that a horse, backed

Who likes a glorious
Days Sport.
I do.
Well then go to Jacksons
Steeple Chase Grounds
on Thursday the 6" of August and
You Will have it
Grand Match again.... .....me
and
Hurdle Races

to a considerable amount was to run twenty miles in an hour with twenty leaps five feet high. The course is almost a mile round so that he had to run twenty times round. The first ten were done within the half hour by four minutes. Off he went again and the interest began to increase. Most people thought he would win, it seemed certain, he had just finished the thirteenth mile and had four minutes, which was plenty of time, for the last, when down he broke suddenly. The people who thought it was finished all rushed round in hundreds cheering. Some called out "Dont stop" others for the jockey to dismount and he would win yet. if he could only get air, there being five minutes wanted to the hour, but the people would cram round, those behind pushing those before, and the owner in a tremendous passion screamed out " I will defend my own horse" and partly with his whip and partly with his horses kicks, he drove them back a few paces. but they closed in directly. The poor animal was quite done up and being unable to stand was supported home by ten men. It was quite dark and we came home in a miserable state of mind from which I dont expect to recover for a week. I dont ever remember feeling so sick as to think of a poor animal being. perhaps killed for the amusement of a crowd of people.

Friday. 8th I went to Roneys for a carmine cobalt and Vandyk brown for Annette. Worked hard on my history all day. I hear how Prince Louis Napoleon with the counts Bertrand, and Montholon invaded France on Tuesday afternoon with fifty men. They landed at Boulogne, and Prince Louis gallantly placed his hat on the top of his sword and rushed down

98

the principal street calling out "Vive l'Empereur" and into a guard-house. The soldiers seemed inclined to join him when an officer darted out and screamed "Vive le roi". A little battle was then got up without much difficulty which without being equal to Austerlitz was nevertheless glorious for the invading army fought desperately until they unfortunately turned round and began, not to run away, but just to try and reach their boats in the quickest possible

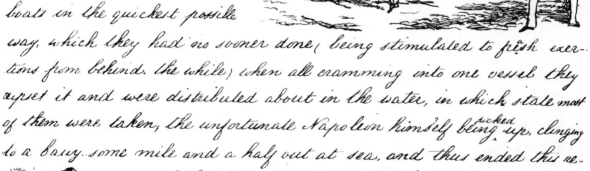

way, which they had no sooner done, (being stimulated to fresh exertions from behind. the while) when all cramming into one vessel they upset it and were distributed about in the water, in which state most of them were taken, the unfortunate Napoleon himself being picked up. clinging to a buoy. some mile and a half out at sea. and thus ended this remarkable business, which must be considered the most extraordinary invasion which has taken place in the annals of man.

Saturday. After Mr Skeel. I went to Finch Lane and got four numbers of the History of France. If any one knew how I restrained myself from buying bottles of ginger beer the whole way down Holborn, they might pity me. for I was actually broiled by the sun

Sunday. Col Shulke came to dinner and I pondered over the History of France for half an hour. Sunday is the only day I can spare to look at it so that I enjoy it beyond anything particularly as I look at it so seldom that the illustration are almost new to me. I could not go out and was desperately tired of not doing anything. I got a head ache

if I drew I got one if I read and I got one with doing nothing. Miss Glanville and Mr Prior came in the evening Miss Glanville sings pretty considerably. and Col Shulthe hearing that Mr Prior had been to Batavia appeared very glad and said he must have a little chat with him

Monday. The King and Queen of the Belgians arrived at Woolwich on Saturday and the Queen was at the French chapel yesterday at nine oclock mass. There is to be a review of the artillery and riffles for their edification on Tuesday.

Tuesday. The Queen prorogued Parliament at a little after two. and I and Henry had the pleasure of walking the whole way with her. The cheering was very great and the crowd greater.

WEDNESDAY. The morning was fine at all events and as this was the day intended to be spent at Mr Bussetts. it was considered a more pleasing circumstance then if it had been pouring rain. A great detachment set out for Hampstead at about one. leaving Henry and I who were to go at four. Now it came to pass that Henry had a pair of boots and I had a pair of boots. One of mine had a hole in it and one of Henrys had a hole in it. I sent one of mine that had a hole in it to a cobbler and Henry sent one of his that

100

had a hole in it to a cobbler. with a strict injunction to have them both done by three. The cobbler said he would. "Three oclock" no shoes. "hallo "four oclock" no boots" come this is carrying the joke too far. The female went in twenty times in half an hour and came back every time say they were not done yet. Five oclock. "no boots" Here Henry and I began to cry

"Hurra" O my goodness" pouring rain "Agony. six oclock, give it up." No (seven oclock). Desperation last chance sent in for the boots to be sent as they were. This may appear a rash step but it should be considered. that we acted under the unpleasant conviction that if we were compelled to stay at home we would starve for everybody being out there was not a chance of our getting anything to eat or drink. Incited by such feelings as these it may readily be imagined that we were not slow in using any means in our power to gain possession of the ill fated boots. and therefore when at a few minutes after seven they were brought in our joy was not unmixed with surprise and even a small particle of indignation. when we found that they were not touched, not a single stick was there in either of them. We determined to go with them as they were. and being favored by the dusk we darted off, think ing it a great deal better fun than if the boots had been sent in done brown at half past one. We past over Primrose hill just as the sun was setting. We arrived at Mr Bassett's at eight and tea being just over the circumstance added considerably to our joy to think that we shoudd have nearly lost our tea a second time. We spent a very pleasant evening. Mr Selous came, and walked a part of the way home with us, and not being able to get a coach, a cab was hailed and all the party but James and I stuffed into it. We set off at a quick trot and reached home a few minutes after the vehicle having met with nothing on the road beyond drunken men at intervals.

THURSDAY. 14: Tutor came at 12 lol Shulke says he wont go till January. The Dancing Envelope has failed in the printing and I have got to do it over again. I would a great deal sooner do anything as large as a Tournament than the size of the envelopes on transfer paper.

FRIDAY. Doing envelopes all day. in the evening went with Ruff to the serpentine

Saturday. Papa made an appointment t° with the lol to Canterbury to day. He said he would be here at half past ten and Papa had been waiting

an hour when at about a quarter to twelve up drove a cab to the door and out jumbed the colonel. He said he was in great haste just going off to Ireland, he had told the servant at Fecours  to call him at half past eight and the fellow did not till ten that he had immediately swallowed a cup of tea called a cab determined to go to America and drove off here in a great hurry and a flat oil skin cap which added considerably to the military appearance of the illustrious man. He regretted exceedingly Papa's having had the trouble of waiting for him but he had determined from some communication he had received to go first to Ireland for about three weeks and from thence to America without delay. He thanked Papa and Uncle in the warmest manner for their kindness and attention to him and concluded by hoping all sorts of things about meeting again, jumped into the cab and drove off.

SUNDAY. Well I am very sorry he is gone. I dont think I ever liked any one so much in so short a time and I cant help thinking he wont come back again at all events not for years once he gets to America.

The day being fine I thought a country walk would not be a bad thing so accordingly Henry Hank Ruff and I set out on the road to Willesden. The day being very fine as I before hinted we were led on mile after mile till we reached Perrivale church.  From this we saw a hill and thinking we might as well get to the top of it we did, and then we saw another and thinking that there must be some very fine views from the top, we reached it and found no extensive view as we had anticipated but a beautiful path through a park Being impressed with the belief that there must be something very remarkable at the other end of it we went on and were certainly repaid by the extreme beauty of the surrounding scenery We were now I should suppose about seven miles and a half from London just then there suddenly appeared the entrance to a a very narrow dark lane so narrow and so dark, that we not having met a person for upwards of two miles, were naturally frightened. We were immediately convinced that if we could only reach the end of that dark lane that something very extraordinary must certainly take place. When we had gone about one mile down the lane the loneliness began to weigh on poor Franks spirits. and he strongly advised turning back. Ruff appeared also of the same opinion. but I imagining that I could see the end of it and Henry imagining the same thing we determined to go on, so I seized up Ruff in my arms and Henry comforting Frank in some other way we pushed on and after about a quarter of an hour quick walking, we were agreably surprised at finding ourselves. within half a mile of Harrow. We all three sat up on a hedge to enjoy the idea and wish to Goodness we had a cold collation and when at last it was time to go home

we actually did not know which way to go. Henry thought that London was that way Frank was certain it was this way and I was positive it was the other. We knew we had come by a much longer way than the high road and it was what we wanted to get a hold off but as there was great danger of our going to Birmingham or some such place if we went in search of it we deemed wisest to go home the way we came, and accordingly got off the hedge on which we had rested for about five minutes, and set off rather melancholy at the idea of having to walk nine miles In a very short time I was made quite fresh again by the beautiful views which met us every instant. Every thing looked twice as well as when we were going: the sun being behind us and it was now that we were repaid for our trouble in going on from one hill to another when we were going, and thinking there must be some very extensive view from the summit which we never appeared to reached. and yet went on on. The fact was that the view was behind us instead of before, as it now appeared, and it was no wonder we did not see it. for altough we looked round repeatedly. for the way was almost all through lanes and it was only from one gate that it could be seen. At all events there it was a beautiful panorama. much better than the view from Hampstead. and it was well worth going the whole way to see. It was here that while passing through a park a rabbit suddenly appeared in the middle of our path. coming towards us. Of course we encouraged in what we thought the most enticing manner that man is capable of assuming towards beasts, such as balancing yourself in a peculiar manner on one leg while the other is held lightly in the air the right hand is held out as if you wished the animal particularly to bite off the first finger and thumb which keep moving in a nervous, at the same time coaxing manner. The expression of the face should be playful and a lamentable attempt at chirping usually accompanies it. The rabbit in this instance did not appear to be captivated by any of these appearances not even by the tempting inducement of a whole finger and thumb but deliberately turned tail and fled in the hedge while the three of us made three distinct terrific grasps at his body. Time wore on and we began to get nearer and nearer home we were just at Maida hill when down came one of the most tremendous showers of rain I ever experienced. We never stopped running till we reached home hungry wet and tired. The two former were soon done away with but the latter took its time and remain-ed all night

MONDAY. The wether has changed horridly. The beautiful clear blue skies of last week have given way to a dull fogged appearance and pours of rain. I am not sorry but I did wish to take a moderate walk to counterbalance the affects of yesterdays. As it is I have been paint-ing all day except at intervals when I went up stairs to touch up the legs of Frank and Charles with an instrument of torture I found in the road yesterday the doing of which besides being sound wholesome exercise for me was calculated to impart a glow of health among the innocents from the lively and brisk manner in which it caused them to skip about, the day being cold

TUESDAY. As soon as Mr Street went. I pounced into the big room and fell on my history with a determination quite imposing, and began playing about on it with various fancy colors. I took up a knife and began to scratch a white horse's back with great violence, not that I was aware of his being troubled with fleas but because it was out of draw-ing and wanted alteration. When this pro-cess had been gone through I nearly rub-bed a mans head off with the corner of my hankerchief. He was a big man and was lying in a horizontal position, a-cross the picture with astonishing coolness considering the two horses who are gallop-ing over him.

WEDNESDAY. I began a new history to day of "Richard cœur de Lion pardoning his brother John." "I pardon him said Richard and wish I could as easily forget his injuries as he will my pardon" so saith the his-tory of England, but I should very much like to know whether he really said it or not. such a thing as that might be so easily invented. though. I dont know, it is almost too fine for that I hope it was not. At all events I began a history called Richard pardoning his bro ther John and if twelve men all stood up on chairs and began speaking at once it would not alter the case. in the least.

Thursday. Tutor will go on coming three times a week and I cant prevent him though I am sure I dont want to prevent him only that some times when I am in a desperate humor to draw I am obliged to go and do my things for him, in the same way. I sometimes get into such a humor for translating that I dont like to go and draw

Friday. I ran out early with Ruff to the serpentine she has grown quite fond of swimming. I have begun to translate the History of France by Theodore Burrette. and find it much more difficult than any French I have done. I am working away at my history like a horse that is like a boy.

Saturday I am just reminded of an anecdote which colonel Shultz told us and which as it would make a good subject for an illustration I will relate. While he was in the dutch service besieging a town in Batavia, the place having been bombarded and taken the soldiers bivouaced in the town at night. The inhabitants who had witnessed the terrible effects of

the cannon impressed themselves with the belief that they were gods and by way of adoring them came in the night and placed all manner of of beautiful fruits and other luxuries on the top of those engines of destruction. This was ill judged on the part of the zealous Batavians. for they ought to have known that the unfortunate cannon must have suffered great mental agony, to see the good natured men coming placing provisions on their backs where they could not reach them, instead of putting them into their mouths. But that would have been as useless perhaps as the other for no sooner had the worshippers gone. when the hungry soldiers delighted at the treat

rushed upon the fruits and devoured them. SUNDAY. 28 The show over Henry Frank and I went into the park and sat on a seat near unto the serpentine. A policeman approached and after first asking if either of us had a pinch of snuff to give him began to enter into conversation in a very extraordinary manner for p policeman. He began by asking which was the most difficult the Latin or French grammar he then went on to speak various small sentences in both languages and lastly to make mathematical figures on the path and explain to us that two halves made a whole..two parallel lines can never meet and other difficult problems

which he explained in the clearest manner possible. He said that he was very tired walking about there half the day and had a very bad head ache that he I somtimes for an occupation took to admiring the beauties of nature

109

but found it two much for him. The learned policeman walked away. From his accent I am led to beleive he was an Irishman.

Friday. 28ᵗʰ. Hard work all day. The Glandvilles are all going away to Abingdon or some such place to morrow morning.

Saturday. They are gone. Henry and I went went to see them off sap. Curious thing it is that though I never cared about them while they were here I cant help being sorry now as they are gone. Mr Selous brought me the first number of his new work The Queen of Granada yesterday. The illustration is capital and the interest intense. I was trying with all my might to get a sheet of imperial on the board for two new histories I am going to begin. Sir Walter Raliegh in the Tower writing the history of the world and the earl of Essex's rebellion in the time of Queen Elizabeth. In the evening Henry I and Frank went down to Rees late Sladdin in the Edgware road to get our wigs cropped. Rees late Sladdin is a facetious person, and kept us laughing the whole time we were there but as fun of that sort never tells well after. I wont repeat any of the numerous witticisms uttered by the

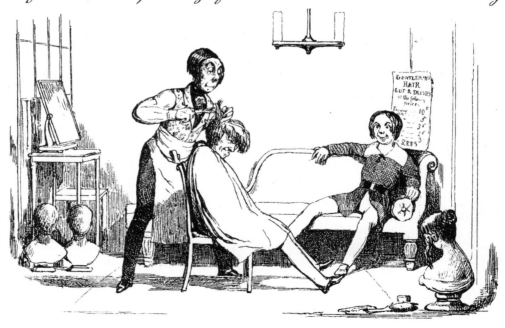

illustrious successor of Aladdin. He has had the shop newly decorated and papered with a green sofa to sit on while you are waiting to be done. A terrific encounter took place to day between Ruff and four swans. It lasted for nearly ten minutes. the four birds hissing and flapping their wings while Ruff screaming barking kept rushing into the water up to his nose. and then running back again.

SEPTEMBER,

UESDAY. Ist",. I was rather at a loss to know what sort of large letter to do at the beginning of this month. but decided after some deliberation that as I have represented myself at the head of the last chapter, in the act of performing with great apparent brilliancy on the violin, it would be only common sense to depict the same distinguished gentleman at his daily occupation of painting

Now perhaps some of the readers of this stuff will recollect that I have displayed myself in a similar situation. on a board in the title page, only that instead of the canvas I am employed in the somewhat degrading occupation of painting a placard on a wall, perched as I have just said upon a board which is supported by two stout poles &

decorated with two reclining ladders, and perhaps those same people may accuse me of imitating my own delectable works. Let me warn those persons that I am perfectly sensible of the similitude of the two productions, and that it is now too late.

Wednesday. Prince Albert yesterday with a large party of fashionables enjoyed the sport of shooting by hundreds all manner of pheasants and par

riges in the preserves of lord Suffield, at some lodge near Windsor.

Thursday. Mr Sheet at half past eleven. out for an hour before dinner In the afternoon began. a new history. of Robert Cecil Earl of Essex the favorite of Queen Elizabeth about to cross the Thames after having embarked in his foolish rebellion which afterwards cost him his life

Friday. The History of France is rather improving in point of illustration I can hardly beleive that the same man could have done some as did others. some are so horribly stiff particularly in the draperies while others are the very opposite. The last batch I got which brings it up to the time of King John of Valois is decidedly the best I have got. I wonder who Jules David is. I never heard of him. Papa thinks. he is the son of the great David

and I dont see any reason why he should not be so I suppose he is
Saturday Yuta came at twelve. painted on Essex. till dinner. transla
ted a page and a half of The history of France. Annette has gone to the
Opera. I beleive it is the Sonambula. the most beautiful of all operas
with exception of Norma.

Sunday. Exactly the same as at least half a dozen other sundays lately
Monday. Went to the palace yard. band played a beautiful set of Musard's Qua.
drilles. the solo parts being performed as at the concerts d'hiver. I declare I
think the cornet a piston player was as good as Laurent. I have not heard
Kœnig yet but I suppose he is the best of all cornets. In the afternoon
we went to Ackermans for a a geure of drawing paper. and saw the eth-
ing of Wilkie picture of the trial of Charles the first. I think when it is
finished it will be the finest historical picture that has appeared for
some time. the subject having greatly the advantage of John Knox

TUESDAY. Glorious. Went to Fores. The envelopes out. There they were, one two three four five six all hung up in the window of Mrs Fores 41 Piccadilly corner of Sacville Street some of them being colored in a very flaming and extraordinary manner. To make the matter worse Dickenson sent for a dozens copies of the Tournament in the afternoon

WEDNESDAY. As sure as I am living there was a critique of the Envelopes in the "Times" this morning and whoever dares to say there was not is a liar. "Hurra".

Thursday. Tutor at 12. Began a new history of the death of Edmund the Pious. Mr Bassett came at ten oclock in the evening to arrange with Papa about Mr O'Farrals house. which he is going to make a drawing of.

Sunday. Mr Selous has given me the second number of his new work The Queen of Grenada. The interest increases and the illustrations are excellent.

Monday. 14". Mr Mayne arrived to day at four oclock from Germany.

Tuesday. My history of the death of Edmund the Pious is nearly finished. in the evening translated a page of the History of France. It appears that Col Shultz has not once been heard of since he left us. though he promised to write a line to say he was safe directly he reached Dublin. Rather odd. Papa has gone to Mr Moore O'Farralls to dinner.

Wednesday. 16 Henry and I were just going off to fetch Mrs O'Connor and Victoire to go the Zoological Gardens with us when just as we were ready downs comes the rain pouring like fun. what that is I dont exactly know. All up with Squeers. Went out in the afternoon and got the toothache.

Thursday. 18° Awake all night, rheumatism in the face. turpentine this morning. quite well. Fine day because we were not going to the Zoological Gardens.

Friday 18th. The morning having a smiling appearance. it was resolved that we should all at an early hour; after having previously decorated our heads with hats and bonnets; repair to the receptacle of wild beasts in the Regents Park. James went for Mrs O'Connor and Victoire but it afterwards turned out that they could not come. We were all in a most uncomfortable state of alarm lest we should be prevented from going a second time by rain. One cloud would keep hovering over the house in a most brutal manner but the fine weather triumphed eventually and we set off without our destination without any disturbance occuring, with the exception of the slight commotion occasioned by Aunts having conviction that we. that we were going the wrong way. The first object that strikes the eye of an observing stranger on entering these grounds is a gravel walk lined with bushes the second a bear pit. let me describe it. The bear pit is as square pit of about twenty feet deep and forty eight in diameter with

a stout wooden pole in the middle. It is occupied as the name implies by bears, to the number of three. the Cinnamon. the brown and the North American black. who either beg for victuals at the bottom of the pole on their hind legs or on their heads at the top. Benevolent strangers place penny buns on the end of poles and hold them out to the interesting creatures with a degree of mildness perfectly paralysing. They sometimes hold out little apples. I had been walking about the gardens for about two hours when a report was spread that the animals (felis   ) were going to undergo the process of feeding which ceremony takes place as the keeper informed us four times a week and then only once in the way. It occupies the space of ten minutes and is performed by in the first place the best part of the leg of a cow attached to an iron hook, fas- to a long stick which with the assistance of a strong arm belonging to a strong man in a velveteen coat is thrust just near enough to the bars of the cage, to place the savage beasts in agonies of expectation, while stretch- ing out their paws as far as they possibly can and roaring dreadfully the while tear in the meat with a ferocity perfectly alarming. Shortly after this as I was walking along the path at the farther side of the Gardens I suddenly came on an elephant kneeling on the grass while a red car was being fasten ed on his back. Some eight individuals including myself got into it and the animal being commanded to get up we were hoisted into the air in a most fearful way and carried about the grounds in that elevated position for the

117

space of ten minutes. The brute carried about large or small parties for upwards of two hours. and as soon as each had had their ten minutes and the keeper cried out "Bite" kneeled down till another party mounted the car. The eagles and

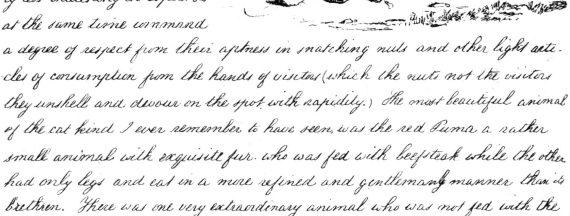

Vultures are a very interesting portion of the collection, at least to me. There is one, the golden crested eagle which is a particularly fine bird. The monkeys are decidedly less interesting in aspect but at the same time command a degree of respect from their aptness in snatching nuts and other light articles of consumption from the hands of visitors (which the nuts not the visitors they unshell and devour on the spot with rapidity.) The most beautiful animal of the cat kind I ever remember to have seen, was the red Puma a rather small animal with exquisite fur. who was fed with beefsteak while the other had only legs and eat in a more refined and gentlemanly manner than its brethren. There was one very extraordinary animal who was not fed with the others. He was sitting on two legs, painting the inside of one of the cages. I

am told that although possessed of such remarkable faculties this species is not at all rare.

Saturday. Victoire came to spend the day and I worked all the morning at Sir Walter Raliegh in the Tower and to make it more interesting writing the history of the wörld. After dinner went into the park and stayed there till tea. Victoire went home at nine. Wednesday 23ᵈ. The princess Augusta died yesterday morning. Sunday. I and Henry went to Mᶜ Moores to ask him what time the last steamer starts for Gravesend to morrow morning. James Papa and he are going together with Mʳ and Mʳˢ Roney and I dont know how many be- sides, to a launch at Chatham which takes place at four. It was arranged that the party were to meet at Hungerford stairs before nine. Henry and I after leaving Mᶜ Moores went up the Hampstead road called at Mʳ Baumers and came across the feilds home

Monday. They went at nine. It rained hard all day and came at about half past ten very wet but after having passed a very pleasant day. Lunch — beautiful.

OCTOBER.

HURSDAY. **1st.** Because this is the first day of the month and therefore ought of all other days to begin with something lively, entertaining or instructive. for that very reason and no other I have nothing to write, that is that I have not written over and over again namely. that I got up in the morning that Mr Street came at his usual hour. that I dined, drew, went out, came in and finally retired.

Friday. 2d. I am compelled to write the word "nothing".

Saturday. 3d. Translated three quarters of a page of the History of France before breakfast Mr Street came at 11; out till dinner, drawing all the rest of the day.

Sunday. 4th. The two Mr delous's came to tea this evening. Mr Angelo brought the second number of The Queen of Grenada. Thank you sir I am very much obliged to you and expect a good read to morrow morning at my breakfast.

Monday 5th. Papa made an important bet with Mr Angelo Selous yesterday evening to the amount of one sovereign namely that there would not be war with France within three months. Mr Selous was willing to stake twenty pounds that there would. The bet was taken down on paper, signed by the parties, and witnessed by. Michael Conan. Jas Doyle and Frances Moore.

James Annette Aunt and Aunt Anne have all gone to the Promenade concerts at the Princess's Theatre which opened the other night under the direction of Mr Willey

Wednesday. Henry and I went to Mr Stephens's with a note from Uncle. He shewed us his pictures among which is a very curious sketch in brown or an etching I dont know which, of Voltaire and a party of his friends, evidently portraits and done from nature,. There is also a most remarkable portrait of Napoleon, when first Consul. He gave Henry and I half a dozen engravings each and a lunch which were both very gratifying to the senses in their different ways.

Thursday. I was walking down Oxford Street this morning, and at the corner of Duke Street I was very much amused by a man who was selling rings. which he called silver, at one penny each. He said that two of the celebrated sporting characters of the day had made a wager while sitting over their wine in one of the large hotels in St James's Street, that the limited number of one hundred silver rings, would not be sold in Oxford Street in one hour. that two umpires were

watching him at that moment to see that he behaved properly. that his directions were not to let them out of sight of the public for one moment; that it was nothing to him whether they bought them or not as he would get well paid for selling them and that was all he had to look to. He concluded by begging the people in the most friendly manner, not to allow themselves on any consideration to be led into the error of the foolish people on London Bridge last year who under the influence of fear, stood looking on when, in consequence of a similar wager one hundred sovereigns were offered to the public at a penny each (here the interesting speaker described in the most poetic terms the manner in which the pennies trembled in the peoples hands like an aspen leaf) and that if the gentlemen present asked their own minds what deterred from buying the ring at once they would find it was fear " Most amusing this.

Sunday. 11th This day will always be remarkable in the annals of history as the first on which Richard Doyle commonly known as Dick, and his brother Henry acted as waiters at a small dinner party in a gentlemans establishment that establishment being their fathers. The case is briefly as follows. Br Rothwell. Mr. Mayne. his mother and his Aunt were invited to partake at six oclock of that pleasant repast termed in modern polite language, a dinner. The female in attendance being one of that interesting race of creatures who on all such occasions allow the breaking of glass and other valuable property not to mention the upsetting of harmless jugs of porter, to occupy by far too much of their time. The services of Dick and Henry Doyle were promptly called into action. The result was perfectly satisfactory, so much so that this extraordinary pair of waiters were at last invited to take a seat at the table much to the consternation of the guests, and in a few moments showed themselves as quick in carrying articles of consumption to their mouths as they had been a minute before in carrying plates from the table

Monday. 18 I went to the palace yard with the avowed purpose of hearing some good music or shivering in the attempt. I had no occasion to do the latter as the band played a very beautiful air from Lucia de Lamamoor "Regnava nel silenzio" is the name I think. Beautiful

Tuesday. There was a long letter in the Times to day to lord Palmerston from Mr Thiers. I dont know what was in it because I did not read it. The danger of a war with France is so great that I am afraid to go out without a walking stick chair That is not the worst for the English navy has been set on fire at Sheerness. There is a gentleman named Safe coming here on Thursday I hope he is what his name implies safe because really in these dangerous times people ought to be particular who they let into the house. I would not be at all surprised if I found myself on fire when I awake tomorrow morning

Wednesday. I went to Chancery Lane for Uncle this afternoon and when I came home found Papa and Uncle just going off to dinner with Mr McEvoy and in want of a cab. It was not thought that there was time to go to a stand so I ran out to watch if one passed but not seeing one what do I go and do but run off to the stand at a space resembling lightening when at its quickest "Jump in cries the cad and

123

I jumped in," Cambridge Terrace" and off he drove. but no sooner was I seated in the vehicle than I began get into a flutter and picture to my mind all sorts of Papas and Uncles coming out of houses and making down public thoroughfares without the aid of cabs. Worked almost to a state of frenzy I popped my head out of the window and beheld the two individuals who occupied my thoughts in the act of crossing over the Edgware road. They saw the cab and hailed it but the man imagining himself engaged would not stop till I dashing my head out of the window and in a voice resembling thunder shouted "Stop". It took affect, the cabman pulled up. I got out at one door while they got in at the other and off they drove.

Thursday. At four oclock Henry and I gave Ruff what might be called a "souser", in a tub that his appearance might be rendered as gentlemanly as possible to night being the night on which a musical practice is to take place. At eight oclock, the light in the hall having previously fallen through the lamp on to the floor and thereby thrown upwards of half a dozen people into a state of the utmost consternation, the two Mr Selous's arrived in company with a roll of music and a claronet and shortly after came Mr Mayne with an Aunt and a Mother then Mr Safe and then Mr McEvoy. These being all lodged safely in the Drawing room, the ceremony of tea began with great spirit. First Henry boldly took up a cup of tea and presented it to Mrs Henn, while I seizing up a plate full of something of the muffin genus darted in pursuit, then Henry caught up another cup and rushed in the direction of Mr Mayne. This game was kept up for more than three quarters of an hour, forming a kind

124

of dance But I must pass over these things and get to the grand trio of Beethoven which was the crack thing of the evening. Every one knows the trio and every one there knows it was never done so well as this evening. Mr Selous sung "When I think on the wrongs he has done one" in first rate style and Mrs Safe sang "O! che in ceilò" in first rate style besides which I must not omit to mention a grand fantasia on favorite airs from Lucia

de Lammermoor which Dick Doyle did _not_ perform on the violin with great brilliancy and feeling but wished very much he could. Now this was all very pleasant and fine, nothing could be pleasanter or finer. At about twelve oclock a supper having contrived to lay itself on the table the multitude hastened to partake thereof Mr Selous being called upon for a song, gave (if I my use the Newspaper language) the immortal Old King Cole, and Mrs Safe being called upon for somthing of the same sort sang "Molly Carew" with great applause, and so the evening ended.

Friday 16th "Nothing".

Thursday I mean Saturday the 17" I have just been having a lesson on the violin and am thoroughly tired in the finger joints. Annette has gone to Drury Lane with Mr Mayne his mother and his Aunt. Pilet the new violincello player is to make his first appearance. I was going down that passage which seperates

the Duke of Devonshires gardens from the Marquiss of Lansdowne, this evening when just as I was about half way up it six men who were in a playful mood came rushing towards us with a terrible noise, the place being not more than four feet wide and the walls on each side very high, the echo was tremendous and Ruff being thrown into a great state of alarm turned about and scampered back with all her might with the men at her heels and just reached the end in time for them to pass her. Of course I had to go back and fetch the animal.

Sunday Show over went out to the Park till dinner. Ruff in very high spirits. Humphreys Clock is getting on a great deal better lately The Old Curiosity shop is intensely interesting and the number for this week particularly well written. I think the characters of Codlin and Short are as comical as any of Boss early works.

Monday. All inspections and exercising are over in the Park now so that when we do go out in the mornings we must be content with Ruffs manœuvres having no others to look at. I was walking across the Park this morning Ruff was with me and for more than half way across, she behaved in the most frolicsome manner that can be imagined. when I reached the Serpentine I turned about in search of the animal, she had shown a disinclination to go into the water for the last few days, and there I saw the merry quadruped standing very deliberately at about three hundred yards off, staring at me, in a very innocent manner, but at the same time expressing very clearly this sentiment, "If you dont come away from there just dont expect that I will be ther myself with following you. Every time I moved towards her, she galloped a little further so that at last she brought me fairly into the middle of the Park. and then it was not worth while to go back again to the Serpentine.

Next to painting music is the most delightful of all pursuits. and as I am learning the violin. I find time to indulge pretty freely in it. though. I am obliged to confess that the chief pleasure, consists in playing the gamut. and if I may judge  from the awful countenances of any one who is unfortunate enough to come into the room at such times. I should certainly be led on to suppose that the sound resembled the singing of an asthmatic donkey or the conversation of an insane cat Notwithstanding this, performers on the violin will sometimes. be charmed with the note that would make a cool listener, turn pale. The fact is that I dont play the scales enough. for instance I determine to play them a hundred times. and when I get to about the sixth time find myself wandering into "Ita Poco" or the grand chorus of priests from Norma.

which for some unfathomable reason I really have a kind of pleasure in scraping. I am told that unless I play from the music it is no use learning and that I may as well give it up. Acting upon this hint I have made out an "andante" two lines long, in Loders book. and I regularly frighten the whole house with it, for half an hour every evening. I feel some degree of curiosity to know when I will be able to perform a grand fantasia on airs from the "Sonambula" with great spirit.

Tuesday 20th. Fencing is all very well in cold weather but not quite so pleasant in warm. The masks are particularly calculated to make the face hot, and more particularly in such weather as this, it being scorching. Notwithstanding this disadvantage, I challenged Henry, this morning to a single combat, it being arranged beforehand that a poke anywhere above the belt was instant death, to the person recieving such a poke, and that the person giving or administering such a poke, was to be proclaimed victor by the unanimous voice of the surrounding multitude. We fought till we were weak, without either so much as grazing the other, and in this happy state of things breakfast was announced and we were led off by the crowd.

Wednesday. Just at the present time we are all busily engaged in considering what we will do for Christmas. It is pretty well decided now. James and Annette will have the "Jeruselem Delivered" quite finished, if they can, besides which Papa has not seen any of what they have been doing for at least two months. I am almost decided on doing a kind of procession which I cant describe, for Papa, and three months of this journal written out clean with illustrations There are some other things which I wish to do, but am afraid I wont have more than time enough to finish the two I have mentioned, particularly if I do the procession as long as I have it in contemplation. In the midst of all these projects I sometimes get into such a wretched state of hating everything I do, that I feel as if I

128

could not go on with any of them. The only thing to do in such cases is just to wait quietly untill I get into a more favorable condition, or to go on, Either is better than committing violence on my person or going into solitary situations like" the cur wot shunned society". I must confess that I have not got into any of these humors with my" Christ- mas things" as they are familiarly called, for the simple reason, that I have not begun them yet, but wait till I do and then I will have plenty. I began the first paper of "The Procession" to day namely the grand band" I am in a great state of anxiety to know whether it will be liked (: I mean the whole Procession when finished) because without boasting I think I may say I never saw anything like it and that make the uncertainty so much greater. Now with such a thing as my Journal it is a different matter. I know that Papa likes me to keep a journal. I think that he would have no objection to my writing it out on clean paper and I hope that the illustrations will not be worse than usual, but the Procession, I don't know whether it wont be considered as nonsense.

Thursday 22°. If I was not going to be an artist I would like best to be an officer in the Life Gaurds. There is scarcely anything so delicious to me as a review and no days in the year I enjoy so much as those on which I go to the Horse guard inspections in Wormwood Scrubbs which generally take

place twice or three times during the season. I would willingly walk twice as far to see one and would never be tired of seeing them.

23d Who is there that will say that the days of chivalry are gone when they hear of the "passage of arms" which took place this day and which I am going to describe. This glorious pastime was perhaps never held in such perfection since the celebrated "Tournament in the plains of Ashby de la Zouche and the "Passage of Arms" under Philip le Harde king of France, the Eglintoun Tournament being decidedly inferior in point of sport, inasmuch as while in the three first, the champions besides charging with the spear, came to close quarters and fought with the sword and mace, in the latter they only tilted over the barrier. The Tourney of which I speak had been announced for several days and altough it was not announced in the public papers, was no doubt privately circulated to an immence extent. The sport unique in all respects had also the charm of complete originality, one of the knights sir Francisco de somthing or other taking the character of Tancred and the other, sir somthing or other de Carlos, that of Argante. The costumes were appropriate Tancred's being a white surcoat with a red cross worked thereon, a visored helmet with three pheasants feathers attached and worsted overalls for the legs of such a color as to resemble mail, lastly

130

a banner on which was emblazoned a lion gules, the arms of the noble knight. Argante wore a white turban with a black visor which being strictly unhistorical was worn for the purpose of making the face of the fierce Egyptian appear dark and ferocious, his surcoat was also white but he wore a broad scarlet sash which contrasted agreeably with the dark visage and white dress. At ten oclock precisely, the Queen of Beauty

having taken her seat on a splendid throne raised on a scaffolding, the champions were announced by a florish of trumpets, and rode into the lists, Tancred from the elevated position in which he sat, striking his crest with considerable violence against the top of the gateway and thereby placing himself in a state of consternation. He however recovered himself bravely and after riding three times round the lists amidst great applause, took his station at the northern extremity. The charging then began with great spirit; the shock when the opponents met resembling a thunderbolt or railroad collision and placing the

131

horses in such jeopardy as to be hardly able to keep their legs. At about the
tenth of these encounters the warriors dropped their lances and seizing their maces
attacked each other with redoubled fury and so well directed and with such good
will were the blows of the valiant Tancred dealt that in the space of a very few min-
nutes. he closed in with his antagonist and fairly dragged him to the ground while
his own horse freed from its rider. rushed frantically about the plain snorting
and plunging. besides expressing his satisfaction by giving vent to a an immence
variety of stranged sounds accompanied by kicks. The combat meanwhile raged
furiously on foot, the impetuosity of the stout Argantes onsets telling with great

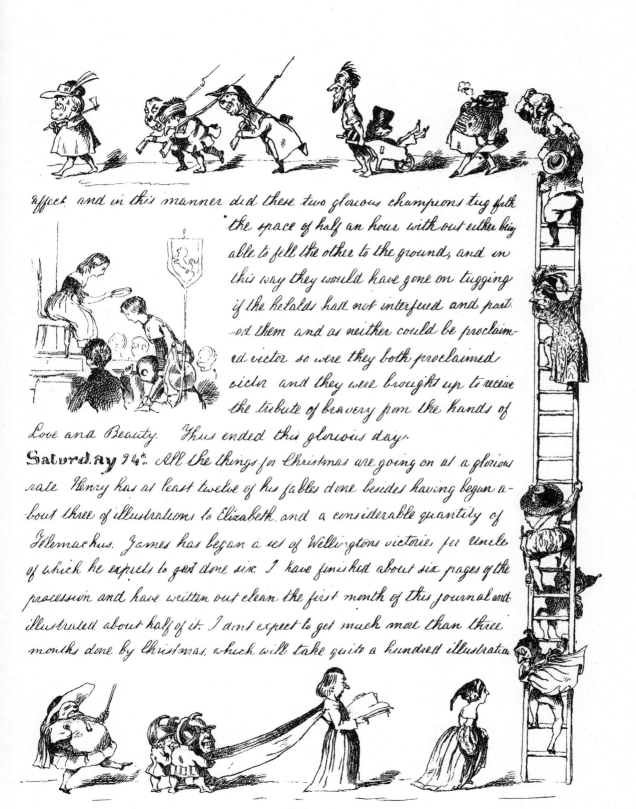

affect and in this manner did these two glorious champions tug forth the space of half an hour with out either being able to fell the other to the ground, and in this way they would have gone on tugging if the helalds had not interfered and part -ed them and as neither could be proclaim -ed victor so were they both proclaimed victor and they were brought up to receive the tribute of bravery from the hands of Love and Beauty. Thus ended this glorious day.

Saturday 14th All the things for Christmas are going on at a glorious rate Henry has at least twelve of his fables done besides having began a- bout three of illustrations to Elizabeth and a considerable quantity of Telemachus. James has began a set of Wellingtons victories for Uncle of which he expects to get done six I have finished about six pages of the procession and have written out clean the first month of this journal and illustrated about half of it. I dont expect to get much moe than three months done by Christmas which will take quite a hundred illustration as for the procession I will get just as much done as I possibly can between between this and then. I only wish the time was twice as long as it is I dont think then I would have nearly time for all the ideas I have got into my head.

NOVEMBER.

Sunday. 1st. At the "show" this morning I had my "history" of the Norwegian soldier defending the bridge of Sandford against the Saxons, which he did for some two or three hours until he fell peirced by a javelin thrown by a soldier from a boat beneath. Papa and Annette at about eleven went by railroad to pay visit to Mr W Stockley and were home at six. Mr Frederick Selous came in the evening and brought a journal he kept when travelling in Switzerland the interest of which is greatly increased by engravings of the principal views &c.

Monday. 2d James and I together are doing an envelope having reference to the Lord Mayor for the completing of which Henry and I on the way to Finch Lane to day went into Guildhall that I might survey those interesting specimens of the antique Gog and Magog which are to be introduced into the envelope above mentioned. When we were on the way home just at Feild Lane Holborn, an inspired divine suddenly appeared on the pavement and without giving any previous notice of his intentions, violently dashed his hat upon the pavement and taking a little volume from his pocket began to preach with a most awfull severity of countenance and and gesture, to three small boys who were all that had as yet collected, and who stood

without understanding a word he said staring up in his face in a kind of stupid astonishment. The best part of the fun has to come yet. Just as we had begun to walk on, our progress was arrested by a particularly angry shout on the part of the preacher and turning round discovered to our surprise that the learned man was bounding about the pavement in a most exciting manner and pointing us out to the congregation who had assembled by this time, as the wicked rich who robbed the poor and did all sorts of other things also. I wonder whether he knew how I restrained myself from buying ginger beer at every cart and shop down that very street some two months ago!

Tuesday 3. The Lord Mayor envelope is nearly finished. Captain Reynolds has written a letter to the Queen, and when I was drawing to day the seat of the chair suddenly fell out and I fell through with such force that I had a good mind not to get up again. Miss Mayne is coming to spend the day the ninth of this month which will be next Monday. I am inclined to this

Wednesday 4th The envelope is finished and gone to the printers. It will come out quite apropos, next Monday being Lord Mayors day. Mr Mayne came this evening

Thursday 5th I was awoke this morning by the frightful screams which usually accompany Guys and while the younger branches of the family rushed with a frantic eagerness to obtain a view of the triumphal procession. I who have long since lost a taste for suchlike historical recollections lay calmly in bed meditating upon what remarkable shapes the faces of the little wretches must be twisted into in their howling. Later in the day as I was crossing Berkley square on my way to the British Gallery to an imposing sight presents itself, a Guy placed gracefully upon the back of a donkey back to back with a novel creature who might have passed for some distant relation of Punch, or even of Judy, but was, I believe intended to represent the Pope. The sarcasm here conveyed was so biting that I quitted the ground instantly, and proceeded to the British Institution where there was an exhibition of the copies of some of the principal pictures from the last Exhibition of the old masters. Francis Moore has got a very good copy in oil of a landscape and figures by Teniers in which there is a sunset background and the shadows going towards it. Titian Velasquez Claude Reynolds, are, among the artists copied.

Friday. 6.ᵗʰ Rain all day. This mornings paper says that the seige of Acre as commenced A meeting was held yesterday some where in Charing Cross for the purpose of raising a subscription for Captain Reynolds when a person named Jones got up and said that he did not wish to mix himself up with the business as he (Jones) being a barrister, had a reputation at at stake (groans) It was said that a thousand pounds had been collected in the city alone but that Captain Reynolds had refused to accept it (cheers). Some one, here asked. timidly what should be done with the money. Mr Jones. Why raise a monument like the Duke of Yorks pillar — eight thousand pounds would do it (cheers).

Saturday. 7ᵗʰ The only thing I find for this day in the manuscript, is "history not finished."

Sunday. 8 Morning spent as usual in the park. Mr Selous came in the evening and brought the third number of the "Queen of Grenada" which has got one of the most beautiful illustrations of the kind I ever saw, namely the lovely Inez in her bower. I dont know any illustrated work now publishing to compare with it, in excellence

Monday. 9th Henry and I went to Finch lane at an early hour. On our way we had the happiness of seeing the unfortunate old Lord Mayor of last year come down the steps of the Mansion house and get into his carriage for the last time to go to Guildhall. We did not wait for the "show" but went on to Clarkes where Henry got in a supply of Fables and got home before two. Mr and Miss Mayne came to dinner and in the evening came both the Mr Selous and Mr Safe. There was some very good music done among which, a duet of Hummel for piano and violin-cello played by Mr Mayne and his sister, was the best. At supper Mr Angelo Selous sung his immortal old King Cole and the "Young Gentleman."

Tuesday. 10th The Civic envelope is out and has printed well. Mr Fores has sent a large quantity of transfer paper, which looks like more business. "Hurra"

138

This is business. I began the Military envelope this morning, finished it by four oclock and sent it off. I am working every evening now as hard as I possibly can at my procession for Christmas. I have given up the idea of getting my journal finished by then, so it is better to try and have the procession quite finished and just show three months or so of the other thing. The Tasso and Henrys Fables are going on at an awful rate.

Thursday. 12th Went to Finch lane for the ten first numbers of the History of France. I never experienced such a November as this in my recollected life. There has hardly been a drop of rain or even a fog on the contrary the skies have been remarkably clear and blue, such as were never seen in November before and although we had a fire in the stove almost all last month, we have not had it once this

Friday. 13 Acre is taken, after a bombardment of about ten hours. Perhaps it would have taken a little longer but that a shell falling into a powder magazine, blew up all

139

the surrounding buildings with some thousands of people among whom were two whole regiments of Egyptian soldiers. On an average there were not two men killed in each of the English ships the ball for the most part falling very much short of them. **Saturday. 14** I really feel afraid I will never be able to put down a quarter of the ideas for my Procession that crowd into my head every time I think of it. Sometimes

after I am in bed at night some idea to my mind more remarkable in point of brilliancy, than any preceeding it, strikes me. I am half determined to get up and put it down but then how am I to get a light, besides dozens of other ideas equally startling no doubt, come pouring into my head and I begin to seriously consider, granting that I manufactured a light, whether I could find time before morning to place them on paper. In this dilemma, after five minutes considera-tion. I have recourse to the following expedient. First jumping out of bed I seize upon a chair, by brute force and plant it in the middle of the floor, becoming possessed of a coat I then place it upon the back of the chair, a pair of trousers in a reclining posture adds to the picturesque effect already produced, and I becoming enraptured at the sight. fetch four boots and place a leg in each but stay something yet was wanting, I seized a hat and placing it on one side of the gentlemans head, gave at once to the whole, a light, cheerful, and even play-

ful appearance. By this time feeling myself rather cold than otherwise, I sprung into bed. Upon awaking in the morning I was immediately struck by the singular appearance in the middle of the room and from thence reminded of the reason that gave rise to it.

Saturday. 15th. After the "show" Henry and I took a walk to Ealing and were home at three Mr Selous came in the evening.

Monday. 16 I began a new history of Boadicea at which I worked till dinner and in the evening did two rows of my procession. Considering how Christmas is I am very much alarmed at the small quantity of it I have done.

Tuesday 17. Two rows of Procession and some of Boadicea before dinner.

Wednesday 18. I tried for about two hours to do a portrait of Charles to day but the more he tried. to smile and look pleasant the more doleful he looked, till at last he began to go asleep, and in that condition was I obliged to do him in

141

the end. Who knows whether I was not magnetizing him all the time, the constant moving of the pencil might have done it for aught I know to the contrary. The life guards and Bliss changed barracks to day They were passing by here, to and from Windsor all day.

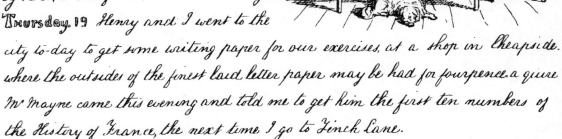

Thursday. 19 Henry and I went to the city to-day to get some writing paper for our exercises, at a shop in Cheapside. where the outsides of the finest laid letter paper may be had for fourpence a quire Mr Mayne came this evening and told me to get him the first ten numbers of the History of France, the next time I go to Finch Lane.

Friday. 20ᵗ This day shortly after three oclock, a Princess Royal was born. huzza!

Saturday. 21 There is no use in us trying to get up any more plays at Christmas because the diference of our sizes would spoil anything serious and I dont believe there is any other very good comic one except The Critic and it requires two many

characters beside being rather like Bombastes Furioso in two or three incidents.

Sunday. 22^d The shows are beginning to decline rapidly, as Christmas draws near and the work for it becomes harder. I have been obliged for the three last Sundays to go on showing my history of Alfred in the Danish camp, just giving a few touches each week by way of a saving clause. As for James and Henry they have not had anything for a fortnight and it is much to be feared that Sunday morning shows, will expire this day at five and twenty minutes to twelve. Of course they will be resumed again after Christmas

Monday. 23^d I drew four pages of the procession to day, and colored two. that I did. yesterday. I am beginning to wish very much that instead of having it in a book with the paper drawn upon on both sides. I had made it in one long strip to roll up or unroll at pleasure because then it would have seemed just twice as long as it does now being done only on one side which is just what I would be glad of for I am tortured with the fear that Papa will think it a little, when finished and I know that if I work day

143

and night till Christmas the volume will still be small. Prince Albert it appears has got a particularly strong predelection for music for not only have all manner of organs been erected, both at Buckingham palace and at Windsor for his use exclusively. but at the Concerts d'Hiver to night will be performed a grand overture to an M S opera composed by his Royal Highness. Beside all this it is confidantly asserted that an easel oil colors canvass and all the etceteras belonging thereunto have been conveyed into the palace and that the illustrious consort of Englands Queen is about to commence a large historical picture. Glorious state of things. What would his Britanic majesty George the Second have said if he had dreamed that his very great granddaughter would connive at her husbands painting a historical picture within

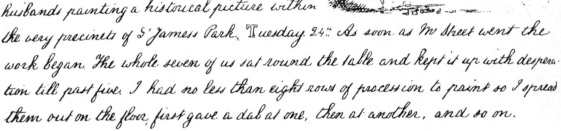

the very precincts of St James Park. Tuesday 24th. As soon as Mr Sheet went the work began. The whole seven of us sat round the table and kept it up with desperation till past five. I had no less than eight rows of procession to paint so I spread them out on the floor, first gave a dab at one, then at another, and so on.

Tuesday. 24th Lord Cardigan will be tried in the house of Lords in January next for fighting duel with Captain Harvey Tuckett. I think he is sure to be acquitted.

Wednesday. 25th After the toiling I usually undergo, both day and evening now, I find great relief in an occasional visit to the palace yard. This morning the selection was particularly good there being the "suone la Tomba" duet from Lucia de Lamamoor, and a set of Musards prettiest quadrilles in which the solos were all done as arranged for the orchestra and beautifully done too. I can not help thinking after all that to try Lord Cardigan for such an offence in a place like the House of Lords is to say the least of it very remarkable for in the first place if he is to be tried at all there is not the least reason on earth why the duke of Wellington Lord Londonderry lord Powerscourt and some half a dozen other Peers. should not be handed from their seats by the Serjeant at arms. and placed at the bar to be tried too I am inclined to think that attempted manslaughter is as crimi- nal in the eye of the law as half manslaughter three quarters of manslaughter or whole manslaughter so that if it is just that Lord Cardigan should be tried it would only

be very illnatured not to show the same distinction to the other noble lords. If I may judge from the cases of the last mentioned gentlemen it would appear that the law is not carried into force against every instance of attempted manslaughter. If I connived at annihilating the existence of a member of the human race say James Harlour Professor, for instance, and was discovered, would not I stand in a very awful position with regard to distant lands. I suspect so. Then why should this distinction be, it looks very much like one person being punished for what the other would not except in the case of Lord Cardigan which is only rendered the more extraordinary thereby, for I can not see that he is more culpable than the Duke of Wellington or the Marquess of Londonderry. In my humble opinion it would be better either to punish all alike without distinction of birth or station, or else not to do it at all. A man is forced by the laws of society on pain of being exposed as a coward, to place himself in the way of being shot dead and if he escapes that of being transported for life. I think the idea is horrible. There are some people who say that instead of duelling a man when he is insulted by another should go and beat him, after the manner of Mr Grantley Berkley I suppose. This is the greatest folly I ever heard for in that case the greatest ruffian that ever breathed could just if he happened to be a very strong man use any person not so strong just as he pleased without their having

146

a chance of redress. Talking of lord Cardigan reminds me that to day I saw a party of his hussars in their new dresses for the first time. I don't exactly know how it used to be before but it strikes one that scarlet would look better with the gold lace than the crimson color they have got. At all events it is a variety and I dare say they look very well

in a regiment though for my own part I prefer the dress of the marquess of Anglesey's regiment to any other hussars I ever saw in the English army.

THURSDAY. 26ᵗʰ Did two pages of procession and two more pictures in my journal which just completes the three first months and I am not going to do any more of it before Christmas as I will have quite enough to do to finish the first mentioned thing If any one besides Papa expects anything from me it will be a dreadful catastrophe for I have not anything to give them, though I have made two or three attempts. Mr Mayne called to day for a copy of the Tournament to supply him with which not being in my power, he departed, and in half an hour afterwards twenty five of those commodities arrived, as good impressions as the very first that were printed. This was cheering and to make doubly so the man at Grafs said that if a thousand copies were printed the last would be as good as the first. I took one to Mr Mayne in the evening and when I came home spent the rest of the evening in designing a Christmas envelope which when done is to be brought out immediately. There are few things in that way so difficult to design as an envelope but I think at last we have got one that will do pretty well.

riday. 27th. In spite of the unpropitious character of the weather for such an excursion Henry Frank and I did go into Kensington Gardens for the avowed purpose of sketching from nature therein. Armed with a determination of this nature, it was not surprising that ere long we should become so wrapt up in our sublime art as to be totally unconscious of the flight of time. This was actually the case, and to such a degree that when we recovered our senses it was nearly dark. We started to our feet for the horrid conviction that the gates were shut at sun set rushed upon all our minds at once, and then made towards the nearest gate at the top of our speed. It was shut. Neither of us said a word but consternation was visible in our looks, we turned about and flew down the long walk to the other gate, — Shut. This was awful. Nothing now remained but to go through the gardens and in the event of that gate being shut to drop off the wall. The walk was an unpleasant one, every instant we expected an athletic ranger to rush upon us, from behind a tree and exterminate us, and in case this did not occur who knew whether a highwayman of savage appearance might not dart out of the very next bush and discharge a brace of pistols at us, without effect and then annihilate us with the butt ends. In either case it would be perplexing to say nothing worse. To make the matter more fearful, just

as we had got to this side of the serpentine, we discovered upwards of one thou-

sand crows walking about in the

moonlight at the waters side. At

last we reached the fatal gate and

found it shut. Nothing now remain-

ed but to drop off the wall. Henry

leaped down first and I seized

Frank under the arms and launch-

ed him over, holding him down as far as I could reach while Henry caught

his feet and lifted him on to the ground. I then sprung down, and when

you consider that it was so dark that I could not see the ground on the

other side I think you will allow that the circumstances were sufficiently ter-

rifying. As for Frank he did not recover the shock for at least three hours afterwards

Friday. 28th. Mr Street at half past twelve. In the evening ran down to the Burley

149

tion arcade to see if there was anything new in Delaportes window. There was not so I came home again and drew two strips of Procession, which was a great deal for one night. I have now altogether done sixteen, not reckoning to-nights.

Sunday. 29th. Shall I confess the fact that I worked hard all this blessed day.

30th. If I am not mistaken this is the last day of the month and such being the case, the fact of Christmas coming in the space of three weeks is forcibly brought to my mind. I hardly think I shall will be able to exist after that period There will be such a contrast between the delicious excitement of the present, and the idleness then, for no matter what, I can not do anything for one week at least after the fatal day. It seems as if I was just able to keep up working till Christmas eve and not one minute more. Notwithstanding the the pleasures of holidays. I must say I feel really happier before they begin, the delicious excitement, as I said before, the immensely hard work, the doubts as to whether Papa will like the things we give him, or not. and the expectation, all combine to place the system in such a ferment, that in comparison with it the holidays are dull.

DECEMBER.

TUESDAY. Whenever a month knows that it is wanted to come as slowly as it conveniently can so sure is it to come at the rate of a black whiskered policeman running with energy after a small youth. This is the present case exactly. December knew well enough that I did not want it to come quickly, there is no mistake in the world about that, not the slightest and then the sneaking worthless wretch from some Satanic motive or another, behaves in a directly opposite manner. I feel that this is an unpleasant subject to dwell upon inasmuch as some persons who may chance to read this, might have a predisposition in favor of the month. I was once attached to it, but the outrage my feelings have sustained has induced me to express my sentiments at any risk. When I ponder upon the debasing and degrading conduct I have described, my imagination forcibly tells me the author of it is like this.

151

Wednesday 2 The hard work has now really commenced. What has hitherto taken place has been a mere farce in comparison to it. Christmas in three weeks "shocking!"

Thursday 3° This morning Annette and I walked to Ackermans to get a quire of drawing paper, and were not home till dark, that interesting phenomenon appeared at about half past three In the evening Uncle declared that he would take any one to Exeter Hall who chose to go with him. Every one else said they would not go, so I said I would, and accordingly did. Aunt Anne however afterwards changed her mind and came with me Uncle was going some where else first and had started

Not surprisingly, the *Journal* is full of allusions to people and events now unfamiliar: the notes below may offer some guidance.

RD = Richard Doyle

Page no.

2   John Frost: a former mayor of Newport and a prominent figure in the Chartist movement. In 1839 he led disaffected colliers and mineworkers against regular troops: 22 Chartists died. Frost was condemned to death but the sentence was commuted to transportation for life; he received a pardon 15 years later.

3   'Boz's new work': *Master Humphrey's Clock*, a weekly periodical. This experimental departure from monthly serial publication did not show the benefits Dickens had expected. Towards the end of April he decided to abandon the *Clock*'s machinery and concentrate on expanding one of the short stories into a full-length serial novel: *The Old Curiosity Shop*. (See p. 126 for RD's approval of the revised scheme.)

3   'Bentley': *Bentley's Miscellany*, edited by Harrison Ainsworth (Dickens had resigned from the editorship at the beginning of 1839).

3   'a Quentin Durward'. RD plans to illustrate a scene from Scott's novel.

4   The 'Tournament': see p. viii of Introduction.

13   John Braham (1774–1856): a popular tenor who amassed and lost a large fortune. The loss forced him to return to the stage and concert-room. His voice would have been past its best by 1840.

14   James Sheridan Knowles (1784–1862): an Irish dramatist. He enjoyed an ephemeral popularity.

18   The sketch at the bottom of the page is incomplete. In the original, Buckingham Palace is pencilled in, with a flag flying and the Marble Arch clearly shown. The Arch, designed by Nash in 1828 as the main gateway to the Palace, was removed in 1847 and re-erected at the north-east corner of Hyde Park in 1851.

22   Count Alfred D'Orsay (1801–52): sculptor, painter, dandy, something of a profligate. He had to flee to Paris in 1849 to avoid arrest for debt.

23   The Queen came of age at 18, on 24 May 1837; RD was 12.

24   An incomplete page; there is no pencilling in the original.

26   The Duke's illness was a recurrence of an attack that had struck him at Walmer the previous November. On 13 February, just a week before RD's entry, Wellington had 'become so ill that on reaching Apsley House it was necessary to lift him from his horse' (Stanhope, *Notes of Conversations with the Duke of Wellington 1831–51*, 1938 edn., p. 215.)

27   William Westall (1781–1850): topographical painter. He illustrated a number of works for Ackermann (see 31 below).

27   Richard More O'Ferrall (1797–1880): in 1840 he was Secretary to the Admiralty. Irish.

27   *The Penny Magazine:* promoted by the Society for the Diffusion of Useful Knowledge. Poetry and popular science and history. Its circulation was over 25,000 a week when it closed in 1845 and had been much greater.

29   'Mr Rothwell': probably Richard Rothwell (1800–68), painter. Irish.

31   'Ackermans': Ackermann and Company, Strand printsellers (see p. 113 for an interior view of the shop). Rudolph Ackermann I (1764–1834) was in large measure responsible for the establishment of lithography as a fine art in England.

33   Charles Kemble (1775–1854) nominally retired from the stage in 1836. On recall by royal command, he gave 12 performances, the last on 10 April 1840.

33   George Bartley (1782?–1858): stage manager at Covent Garden 1829–43.

38   Henry Petty-Fitzmaurice, 3rd Marquess of Lansdowne (1780–1863), was President of the Council. The house, originally Shelburne House, is the work of Robert Adam *c.* 1762–8, now much altered: a drawing-room and the dining room have been removed and re-erected in American museums.

38   Bude-light: a type of lamp using oxy-hydrogen gas.

39   'Phiz' (Hablot Knight Browne) and George Cattermole provided the majority of designs for the *Clock*.

39   'Lord Semour': Edward Adolphus Seymour, 12th Duke of Somerset (1804–85). In 1839 he was appointed Secretary to the Board of Control.

40   Below the last line on the page RD began to pencil a heading for the new month, April. In the original, the next two folios are blank except for pencil rulings and the beginnings of a pencilled sketch.

42   'Mr Harding': possibly James Duffield Harding (1798–1863), landscape painter and lithographer. His 'Sketches at Home and Abroad' (1836) earned him a breakfast service of Sèvres china and a diamond ring from Louis Philippe, to whom the work was dedicated.

44   'Mr Mayne': possibly Richard Mayne (1796–1868), 4th son of the Irish judge Edward Mayne (who had done much to help the young John Doyle). Richard Mayne was one of the Joint Commissioners of the Metropolitan Police from the force's inception in 1829, becoming Chief Commissioner in 1850.

45   Chapman and Hall's was at 186 Strand. Booksellers' men and boys are collecting the third number of the *Clock*.

45   See p. x of the Introduction for comment on the Paddington booking-hall.

46   The railway line to Ealing opened on 4 June 1838. Ninepence was the full second-class adult fare for the journey – just under six miles.

46   Richard Gould was tried on 14 April for the murder of John Templemann. The evidence, though strong, was circumstantial and he was acquitted – only to be re-arrested by the police and tried and convicted of burglary.

46   Perivale church: a simple aisleless building of rubble and flint, the earliest parts probably thirteenth-century. It remained very secluded until the mid 1920s.

47   An 'ordinary': a public, fixed-price meal served at an inn or eating-house.

48   The Polytechnic Institution, 309 Regent Street and 5 Cavendish Square, was incorporated in 1838 'for the advancement of the Arts and Practical Science'. Admission was a shilling.

50 Chantrey's large studio was in effect a showroom, containing casts of most of the sculptor's work: a sort of gallery of great men. Chantrey was by this time one of the richest artists in Europe.

52 Sir Martin Archer Shee (1769–1850): portrait-painter, President of the Royal Academy. Irish.

52 Italian Opera House: the Opera House, Haymarket, one of the largest theatres in Europe.

55 The Royal Academy, originally at Somerset House, held its first National Gallery exhibition in May 1838. It moved to Burlington House in the 1860s.

57 Charles Hancock (c. 1795–?): he frequently exhibited his pictures at the Royal Academy. More prosaically, he contributed racehorse portraits to sporting periodicals.

59 The Elgin marbles were amongst the most popular of the British Museum's exhibits. Sir Robert Smirke's new Museum building was still far from finished and RD would have seen the old Montagu House (progressively demolished 1841–8 to make way for the famous great southern façade).

63 'Henry had a copy of the Crew of the Medusa on the raft': after Géricault's *The Raft of the Mendusa*.

74 RD has presumably forgotten to copy Thursday's entry from his draft.

77 Faint pencillings in the original above the sketch.

78 In the original, two blank folios follow.

83 'unfortunate earl of Derwentwater': James Radcliffe (1689–1716), 3rd Earl. A Roman Catholic, he joined the Pretender in 1715 and was beheaded for high treason in the following year.

85 'Tippoo Saib': Tipu Sahib; see 86 below.

86 Seringapatam: the fortress-capital of the sultans of Mysore. During the fourth Mysore war it was besieged and captured (May 1799) and Tipu Sahib, the sultan, killed in the fighting. The victory established British supremacy in southern India.

89 Fores previously exhibited a copy of RD's 'Tournament' in his window (see p. 66). For a note on the envelopes see the Introduction, p. viii.

93 'Francis Moore asked us to go with him to Mr Shaws': Henry Shaw (1800–73), architectural draughtsman, engraver, illustrator, antiquary. *Dresses and Decorations of the Middle Ages* appeared in 1843.

94 Four blank folios follow in the original.

98 Louis Napoleon's 'invasion' was presaged by his Strasbourg adventure (1836) and publication of *Des Idées Napoléoniennes* (1839). The future Emperor of France was at this stage in his career little more than a figure of fun in the popular imagination. After Boulogne he was imprisoned in the fortress of Ham, which he walked out of disguised as a builder's labourer in 1846.

100 'The King and Queen of the Belgians': Leopold I (1790–1865) was Victoria's uncle; he had married the eldest daughter of Louis Philippe in 1831.

113 Interior of Ackermann's shop: see the Introduction, p. x.

115 'All up with Squeers': Squeers of *Nicholas Nickleby*, presumably (the novel had finished serial publication the previous October).

115 The Zoological Gardens were incorporated in the Regent's Park scheme at an early stage. The Menagerie from the Tower of London was absorbed in 1834.

119 Princess Augusta Sophia (1768–1840), the sixth child of George III.

120 John Doyle's bet with Mr Selous is a good indication of the severity of the crisis: Palmerston's blunt handling that summer of the Eastern Question and France's paranoid belief that she was the object of encirclement brought Anglo-French relations to their most dangerous point since Waterloo.

122   In the original, at the foot of the page, is a pencil sketch of what appears to be a group round a table.

127   'Loders book': John David Loder (1788–1846), Professor of the Royal Academy of Music. The book is probably the *General and Comprehensive Instruction Book for the Violin* (1814), a standard work.

134   In the original, two blank folios follow.

136   Captain Reynolds. The story behind this and further allusions (see pp. 137, 145) is, briefly, this: in May 1840 Lord Cardigan – in command of the 11th Hussars – ordered the arrest of Captain Reynolds for placing wine on the mess-table in a black bottle instead of a decanter; shortly afterwards he met another Captain Reynolds, whom he also had arrested, this time for impertinence. A garbled account of these events appeared in the *Morning Chronicle* and Cardigan challenged the writer, Captain Harvey Tuckett, to a duel. Tuckett was wounded. Cardigan, forced to face trial, elected to be tried by his peers, who in less than a day rid themselves of any embarrassment by acquitting him on a technicality of law.

136–7 For a comment on the Guy see the Introduction, p. xiii.

137   Siege of Acre: the success of this siege (see pp. 139–40) forced Mehemet Ali, France's protégé, to abandon his Syrian conquests (see note to p. 120 above).

142   The Princess Royal was Victoria Adelaide Mary Louisa (1840–1901). She married Prince Frederick William, later becoming the German Empress.

144   The pencilled figures beside the easel are Albert – with palette and brush – and Victoria.

145   Cardigan's duel and trial: see note to p. 136 above.

146   'beat him, after the manner of Mr Grantley Berkley': George Charles Grantley Fitzhardinge Berkeley (1800–81), huntsman, notorious for the indiscriminate use of his whip. In 1836 in an attempt to discover an offending reviewer's identity he beat up a magazine proprietor in Regent Street.

152   In the original, the broad outlines of this final sketch are pencilled in.